THOMAS COOK
Travellers

ROME

BY
PAUL DUNCAN

Produced by AA Publishing

Written by Paul Duncan

Original photography by Jim Holmes

Edited, designed and produced by AA Publishing.
© The Automobile Association 1995.
Maps © The Automobile Association 1995.

A CIP catalogue record for this book is available from the
British Library.

ISBN 0 7495 0955 4

The contents of this publication are believed correct at the time of
printing. Nevertheless, the publishers cannot accept responsibility for
any errors or omissions, or for changes in the details given in this guide
or for the consequences of any reliance on the information provided by
the same. Assessments of attractions, hotels, restaurants and so forth are
based upon the author's own experience and therefore descriptions given
in this guide necessarily contain an element of subjective opinion which
may not reflect the publisher's opinion or dictate a reader's own
experiences on another occasion.
**We have tried to ensure accuracy in this guide, but things do
change and we would be grateful if readers would advise us of any
inaccuracies they may encounter.**

Published by AA Publishing (a trading name of Automobile Association
Developments Limited, whose registered office is Norfolk House,
Priestley Road, Basingstoke, Hampshire RG24 9NY. Registered number
1878835) and the Thomas Cook Group Ltd.

Colour separation: BTB Colour Reproduction, Whitchurch, Hampshire.

Printed by Edicoes ASA, Oporto, Portugal.

Cover picture: the Vatican and the River Tiber
Title page: Piazza Navona
Above: Vatican guard

Contents

About this Book

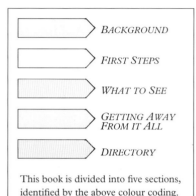

BACKGROUND

FIRST STEPS

WHAT TO SEE

GETTING AWAY FROM IT ALL

DIRECTORY

This book is divided into five sections, identified by the above colour coding.

Background gives an introduction to the city – its history, geography, politics, culture.

First Steps offers practical advice on arriving and getting around.

What to See is an alphabetical listing of places to visit, interspersed with walks.

Getting Away From it All highlights places off the beaten track where it's possible to relax and enjoy peace and quiet.

Finally, the **Directory** provides practical information – from shopping and entertainment to children and sport, including a section on business matters. Special highly illustrated features on specific aspects of the city appear throughout the book

St Peter's is the largest church in the world and Catholicism's most sacred site of pilgrimage

BACKGROUND

Now I have arrived.
I have calmed down and
feel as if I had found
peace that will last for my
whole life.

GOETHE, on arrival in Rome
Italian Journey,
1786-8.

ROME ENVIRONS

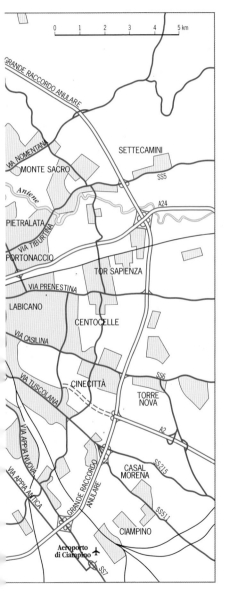

Introduction

*R*ome is one of the most beguiling – and astonishing – cities in Italy. For 3,000 years, from the Etruscan Kings to Mussolini, this city, founded in fratricide when Romulus killed his twin Remus, has survived being burned, sacked, conquered, looted and occupied. Nowadays its cobbled streets resound to the tramp of the feet of tourists anxious to see for themselves the monuments to cruelty and corruption, the scenes of heroic endeavour or unholy depravity, and the sublime examples of human creativity in the museums, galleries, streets and squares. 'What a place!', said Aldous Huxley in 1921. 'It inspires me utterly and inside out.'

For the uninitiated the very idea of Rome, with its wealth of art and architecture, ancient remains and myths and legends, can be overwhelming. A succession of ruins, statues, paintings, galleries, museums can add up to blisters, aching calves and weariness leading to a deadening of the spirit of discovery. The remedy? See just a little at a time.

Take it easy

You are not obliged to devote your visit to the history and culture of Rome, fascinating though these are. There is nothing to prevent you dedicating your time to shopping or the pursuit of gastronomic treats – or passing a few days just idly lazing in cafés, watching the world go by. One of the pleasures of Rome is simply to imbibe the spirit of an ancient city. If there is a moon, nothing can beat a quiet, traffic-free wander at the dead of night around the edge of the Forum.

History

753BC
Legendary foundation of Rome by
Romulus, first of seven kings.
565BC
Traditional date of construction of
Servian Wall by Servius Tullius
(c.578–535BC), sixth of the kings.
510–509BC
Expulsion of the kings and foundation of
the Republic.
451–50BC
Publication of the Twelve Tables, a
codification of the law.
390BC
The Gauls sack Rome.
264-146BC
The three Punic Wars against Carthage
(264–241, 218–201 and 149–146BC)
end with Rome dominant in whole
Mediterranean region. In the second,
Hannibal pre-empts Rome's offensive on
Spain and Africa by marching over the
Alps into Italy (losing thousands of men
and most of his war elephants).
82BC
Sulla becomes Consul heralding a period
of brutal dictatorship.
73–71BC
Slaves' revolt under Spartacus.
60–44BC.
The first Triumvirate (Julius Caesar,
Pompey and Crassus) ends with Caesar
(102–44BC) as sole ruler; his rise to
power marks the end of the Republic.
27BC
Augustus becomes first emperor. Beginning
of a golden age of building and Roman
culture (Virgil, Livy, Horace and Ovid).
AD42
St Peter comes to Rome.
64–67
A great fire in Rome is blamed on

Christians by Nero, whose persecution of
them leads to martyrdom of St Peter
(crucified upside down) and St Paul
(beheaded).
72
Colosseum begun by Vespasian.
270
Aurelian Wall begun as defence against
barbarian invasion.
284
Roman Empire divided into East and
West by Diocletian.
312
Constantine wins control of empire at
battle of the Milvian Bridge.
326
Building of first St Peter's by Pope
Sylvester I. By 337 Rome's population
reaches over a million.
381
Theodosius makes Christianity official
religion.
410 and 455
Sack of Rome first by Alaric's Goths, then
the Vandals; 120,000 inhabitants remain.
476
The Goth leader, Odoacer, becomes
ruler of Rome after displacing the last
emperor, Romulus Augustulus..
590–604
Pope Gregory the Great begins papal
intervention in politics.
800
Charlemagne crowned Holy Roman
Emperor in Rome. City's population is
40,000.
880–932
Rome is ruled by two women – Theodora,
then her daughter Marozia. Powerful
local families vie for the papacy.
1084
Southern Normans sack Rome.

1200

Rome defies pope and emperor to become independent commune.

1309

Papacy moves to Avignon; Rome loses political importance.

1347–54

Cola di Rienzo tries to establish a demo-cratic Roman republic, but is assassinated.

1348

Black Death.

1377

Papacy returns from Avignon.

1417–31

Papacy of Martin V ends the Great Schism in the Church.

1452

Demolition of old St Peter's begins.

1492–1503

Papacy of the notorious Borgia pope Alexander VI. Rome now in full rebirth. Population 50,000.

1503–21

Popes Julius II and Leo X commission important works from Bramante (new St Peter's), Michelangelo (Sistine Chapel decoration) and Raphael (Vatican Stanze).

1527

Sack of Rome by Charles V; buildings destroyed, treasures stolen.

1534–49

Paul III, first Counter-Reformation pope; Michelangelo becomes architect of St Peter's.

1555

Jewish Ghetto instituted.

1585–90

Pope Sixtus V initiates Rome's urban redevelopment.

1626

New St Peter's consecrated and Rome is now undisputed artistic capital of Europe.

1644–56

Bernini redesigns much of Piazza Navona and work starts on his colonnade in front of St Peter's. Rome's population 120,000.

1762

Trevi Fountain completed.

1797 and 1809

Napoleon captures Rome. Annexes the Papal States 12 years later, taking Pope Pius VII prisoner.

1848

Nationalist uprising in Rome; Pope flees and a Republic formed.

1860–1

Garibaldi and his 1,000 followers take Sicily and Naples; kingdom of Italy founded, with capital in Turin.

1870

Royalist troops take Rome. Italy is unified with Rome as capital; Pope's political power confined to Vatican.

1922

Fascists march on Rome; Mussolini prime minister.

1929

Lateran Treaty creates Vatican State.

1943–6

Allies liberate Rome; Mussolini executed (1945); Republic of Italy established (1946).

1957

Treaty of Rome signed, establishing the European Economic Community.

1960

Olympic Games in Rome. Population 2 million.

1975

Census shows 3,600,000 inhabitants.

1978

Murder of ex-prime minister Aldo Moro by left-wing Red Brigade terrorists.

1981

Assassination attempt on Pope John Paul II in St Peter's Square.

1990

Soccer World Cup held in Rome.

1994

A right-wing alliance wins the first elections under a new electoral system.

Roman Empire, 31BC–AD476

*T*he Roman emperors ruled over one of the greatest multi-racial states the world has ever known, whose influence touches our own lives to this day. The date AD476 is generally given as the empire's final year, when Romulus Augustulus, who ruled for a year, was deposed. Only the principal emperors are listed below.

Augustus (31BC–AD14)
Rome's first emperor. His long rule engendered unprecedented stability, security and prosperity which lasted for more than 200 years.

Tiberius (14–37)
Autocratic stepson of Augustus. During this period, Jesus Christ was crucified in Jerusalem.

Gaius or Caligula (37–41)
Remembered mostly for his versatile sex life. Thought to have been mad.

Claudius (41–54)
Handicapped by ill-health, this nephew of Tiberius was a considerable scholar. He developed Rome's civil service and added several provinces, including Britain (AD43), to the imperial swagbag.

Nero (54–68)
Held responsible for the Great Fire of Rome (Christians were blamed, then executed, their number possibly including Saints Peter and Paul). Committed suicide having been condemned to death by the Senate.

Vespasian (69–79)
Fell into disfavour with Nero for falling asleep while the latter sang, but lived to rule for ten years. He enjoyed rude health, had a scurrilous sense of humour and achieved notoriety for his methods of raising taxes. His rule is marked by solid application of the ideals of hard work and good government.

Titus (79–81)
Son of Vespasian. His reign witnessed Vesuvius's eruption which buried Pompeii. The Colosseum was completed, while the Baths of Titus provided the model for those of Trajan, Caracalla and Diocletian.

Domitian (81–96)
Brother of Titus, this savage monster was one of the best administrators ever to govern the Empire. He staged costly public shows and built on a grand scale.

Trajan (98–117)
Important military campaigns extended the Empire beyond the Danube. His reign is

Emperor Augustus with his wife Livia

characterised by feverish building activity. Historian Dio Cassius says that he was devoted to boys and wine.

Hadrian (117–38)
In his travels about the empire he spread the civilising influence of Rome. Much influenced by the Greek tradition, he built the great villa at Tivoli, and rebuilt the Pantheon.

Antoninus Pius (138–61)
Built new harbours, bridges, baths and amphitheatres; during his rule Rome became the most magnificent city in the world.

Marcus Aurelius (161–80)
The Philosopher Emperor. He spent much of his reign at war, but also wrote Meditations , a compendium of his philosophical musings while on campaign.

Commodus (180–92)
Bloodthirsty son of Marcus Aurelius. Blessed with sinister good looks, he loved to don a lionskin as Hercules and slaughter animals in the arena.

Septimius Severus (193–211)
Made his mark as an outstanding imperial builder. His rule, warlike and autocratic, saw solar worship threaten the entire Roman pantheon.

Caracalla (211–17)
Brutal elder son of Septimius Severus, he saw himself as an incarnation of the Sun-god. He granted Roman citizenship to nearly all inhabitants of the Empire.

Aurelian (270–5)
His rule helped the Empire to recover

Visitor to Britain: Emperor Hadrian

from the chaos that had threatened to engulf it. A by-product was the defensive wall built to protect Rome from sudden attack.

Diocletian (284–305)
Divided the Empire into east and west (the Tetrarchy system of government). Much building activity in Rome and elsewhere, and persecution of the Christians as never before.

Maxentius (306–12)
Drowned at the famous Battle of the Milvian Bridge (won by Constantine the Great); instigator of the great Basilica of Maxentius in the Forum..

Constantine I the Great (306–37)
The first Christian emperor, he was an excellent general. His two greatest decisions – to move his capital from Rome to Constantinople and to base his policy on Christianity – were of supreme importance for the future of the Empire, the Christian Church and western civilisation.

Theodosius the Great (379–95)
Christianity became the Empire's official religion. After his death the empire was divided for ever and Rome fell to various invaders.

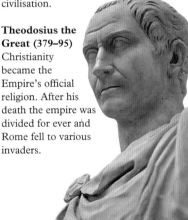

Life in Early Rome

*B*elow is a brief outline of certain key aspects of life in antiquity, known to us from texts by contemporary writers and from sites such as Pompeii.

Dress

The only real distinctions in dress were between rich and poor. Every freeborn Roman male had the right to wear the toga, a semi-circular-shaped garment held in place with pins, tucks or belts and normally worn over a sleeveless tunic. The working-class male wore a simple, short tunic. The toga worn by important officials or boys under sixteen had a purple stripe. After the age of sixteen, boys wore a plain toga called the *toga virilis*.

The female equivalent was a *palla*, a shawl-like garment draped around the shoulders and often drawn over the head, worn with the *stola*, a tunic-like garment. Free-born women wore their hair long: during the Republican era it was gathered in a bun or pony-tail, and in the Imperial age forced into incredible gravity-defying creations. Make-up was applied with the aid of a little hand mirror of blown glass laid over a sheet of metal.

Marriage and Sex

Many brides never met their husbands until their wedding day. Marriage was a business transaction; the bride-to-be had no say in the matter, and was simply transferred from her father's home to that of her husband. Because the whole event was imbued with a sense of ritual abduction, during the marriage itself the bride would 'retreat' into the arms of her mother only to be 'forcibly' removed from them. Before being carried over the threshold of her new home, the bride would smear the doorposts with oil and fat and wreathe them in wool.

During the Empire, contrary to popular belief, the Romans were paralysed by prohibition. A true libertine was one who made love during the day (traditionally only done by

Medallion on the Arch of Constantine; moved here in the 18th century, it came from one of Hadrian's buildings

newly weds), or without darkening the room, or to a woman who was totally naked (by definition a fallen woman - even the prostitutes in Pompeii's bordellos kept on their veils according to surviving mural paintings). The use of slaves for unorthodox sexual practices was regarded as legitimate. Amorous passion was something to be feared: it reduced the man to a woman's slave. Hence, for men, sex with boys was permissible since it was thought to induce a tranquil pleasure which left the soul unruffled.

Slavery

People became slaves because they were children of slaves or were captured in war, though in Rome you also went into slavery if, as a convicted criminal, you were condemned to hard labour. As artisans, agricultural labourers, domestic servants, slaves did all ancient Rome's donkey work. Their childbearing was like the breeding of livestock – the master rejoiced when his herds increased.

Religion

Religion was a set of cult practices, executed officially by a representative of the state or privately within the family circle, as a contract between the human and divine parties. The person fulfilled his obligations in the expectation that the gods would do likewise. Roman religion had certain things in common with other Mediterranean religions: admission by initiation rites; teaching of the good and proper way to live one's life; and judgement after death ensuring eternal salvation or punishment. The most highly worshipped deities were Jupiter, Juno and Minerva, then came Apollo, Mars, Vesta, Venus, Hercules and the goddess Roma.

A barbarian flanks a bas-relief thought to depict a scene from Marcus Aurelius's wars

Death

Funerary rites were designed to ensure the smooth passage of the soul into the afterlife. Hermes would accompany it to the River Styx, where Charon would ferry it either to Hades, the Underworld, or to the Blessed Islands. The body was laid out by the women of the family, washed, anointed and wrapped in a shroud, a coin in its mouth as payment to Charon. Relatives gathered in the house to mourn, the women wearing black as a sign that they had become tainted by association with death. The corpse was finally carried on a bier or cart to the tomb.

Politics

*I*talian politics are in a tremendous state of flux. As politicians across the whole political spectrum fell like ninepins under accusations of corruption in the early 1990s, a new era was born in which, it was hoped, there would be a fresh moral atmosphere. This has been called the Second Republic.

The political parties who shared in the various ruling coalitions since the end of World War II have all been disgraced. In 1993 electoral reform was introduced, aimed at preventing the stalemate in politics that prevailed over past decades. The election of March 1994 resulted in victory for a right-wing alliance of three new parties: the Forza Italia led by media

baron Silvio Berlusconi, the federalist Northern League and the fascist-led National Alliance.

Rome is the centre of all this turbulent activity. It contains the official home of the President of the Republic (Palazzo del Quirinale, see page 67), and is the location of Italy's two houses of parliament, Palazzo Madama and Palazzo Montecitorio – see page 66.

Rome the Capital

Rome has been the capital of Italy ever since the country was united in 1870. Today, not only is it Italy's most populous city but also its largest. And yet Rome is not by any means the economic centre of the state. That is Milan's role. This is not surprising, for Rome's reputation as an inefficient, sometimes inert, bureaucratic mire is well deserved – as anybody who has ever tried to get anything done there will agree. It suffers, possibly, because it is the focus for southerners who, wanting to move away from the economically backward south, move 'Romewards' in search of jobs – which are provided for them in an already heavily-laden government service.

Turin (which for centuries, like Naples, was in continuous use as a capital city) might have made a better capital for the Italian state, but it does

Symbol of power: guarding the entrance to the Palazzo Madama

TANGENTOPOLI

This word relates to the extraordinary series of backhanders paid by big business to politicians in return for favours. While everyone has 'known' about this for years, only recently has the issue been forced into the open and exposed as corruption. As a result judicial investigations have begun into the affairs of some of Italy's most powerful politicians. Dozens of arrests have been made, some followed by suicides. The ultimate goal is a total purge of the system and its replacement by reformed political, judicial and administrative procedures. Not since the war has Italy embarked on such a radical course of reform..

1985 redefinition of the Pact, Catholicism ceased to be the official state religion. Even so, the Vatican is still Rome's other political powerhouse. It has its own government, statutes and head of state – the Pope himself; it issues postage stamps, has its own currency, and cars registered here have Vatican licence plates. The vast Vatican civil service provides jobs for ordinary Romans. In its current incarnation this administration, which includes church officials from nuns to cardinals, looks after what remains of an empire that has been in existence for two millennia. Citizens of Rome have a love-hate relationship with the Vatican.

not have the significance of Rome. Not only is the latter situated halfway between northern and southern Italy, between industriousness and sophistication and spectacular lethargy married to economic backwardness, but it has tremendous symbolic power. Historically, Rome was the centre, and powerhouse, of the ancient world, and it is still the headquarters of the Catholic church.

City of Rome v the Vatican City

Spread over a few hectares 'on the other side of the Tiber', the Vatican State is all that remains of the supremely powerful former Papal State, abolished at the unification of Italy. The 1929 Lateran Pact between the church and state reconciled the two but, after the

A constant reminder of the way things might have been

ITALIAN CHIC:

To outsiders all Italians – and the Romans in particular – are astonishingly stylish. From the fur coated signora buying her vegetables in Campo dei Fiori to the female traffic warden with her gorgeous long hair and heavy gold bracelets, Italians deplore anyone who dares to flout the bella figura code.

This concept decrees that even if you are not worth a million bucks you should make an effort to look as if you are. With fake tans, big fake jewels and even bigger hairstyles adorning often overdressed women, it is sometimes difficult to tell the duchesses from the shopgirls out in the street

Cutting a *bella figura* applies to children, teenagers and men as well, but on a less exaggerated scale. In fact

Italian men have a horror of standing out from the crowd and – in the way they dress at least – are quite conservative. They all look alike: if maroon blazers are the season's dropdead chic, everyone has one. Wear yellow and they will laugh you off the sidewalk. One thing is certain: if you want to belong, follow the herd.

What is the most commonly encountered accessory on a walk in the street? Not hat, handbag or umbrella, but a cellular telephone. Since Italians are born communicators, there has been an apparently unstoppable boom in telefonini: 1.1 million were rented out in 1993. In Rome they are everywhere – even the girl in the plaid suit zooming past on her moped is chatting on hers. It provides a novel outlet for long, loud

BELLA FIGURA

Far left: smart transport, the traffic jam buster
Left: smart but casual
Right: the portable phone – never leave home without it
Below: homeward bound

chatter, and, for the moment at least, there is a certain status attached to owning one. It's that bella figura notion again.

Geography

Rome covers an area of 1,500 sq kilometres, and is Italy's third largest industrial conurbation. With over 3 million inhabitants (compare this with a population of just over 200,000 before the city became the nation's capital 125 years ago) it is also Italy's largest city. Nowadays Rome's population is increased considerably by the influx of non-Italians - mainly Filippinos, East Europeans, Somalians, Ethiopians and North Africans – some of them legal immigrants, most not.

Rome is an immensely popular tourist destination with over 1,300,000 visitors a year. This puts great pressure on the city. Not only is it drowning in pollution, which has long surpassed generally acceptable rates (carbon monoxide and other air pollutants are ten times the maximum limit), but attendant on this chaotic city's expansion are all the problems brought on by too much traffic (though non-essential traffic is now banned from the city centre),

unemployment, drugs and inadequate housing.

Topography

Rome's most distinguishing topographical features are the River Tiber (Tevere) whose banks it straddles, and the various hills over which the city has evolved and developed since the days of the legendary twins Romulus and Remus. All around, the Roman Campagna stretches away to the volcanic hills and the Tiber Valley in the north, the Alban Hills in the south, the Apennines in the east and, in the west, the flat country which runs down to the sea passing on the way Ostia Antica, Rome's ancient port (see page 126).

River ...

The Tiber has its source beyond Arezzo in Tuscany. It wends its way south to Lazio via Perugia and Todi, and by the time it reaches Rome it is a swirling, fast-moving mass of murky water. In the past it flooded the city from time to time – in 1598 it rose 10 metres.

The river and its island – Isola Tiberina (see page 54) – are the reason why Rome was founded on this spot: this was the only place hereabouts where the river could be crossed with ease. Indeed, according to legend the flooding Tiber threatened to drown the twin babies

LOCATOR

From the Apennines of Tuscany, the Tiber sweeps south through Rome towards the Tyrrhenian sea

Romulus and Remus, marooned on its marshy shore, when they were found by the she-wolf who nursed them.

The Tiber may be polluted today, but this does not deter a handful of enthusiastic fishermen from trying their luck with rod and line, while canoeists take to the water. But the river is an under-used facility - quite in contrast to tradition. In the past it was a well-used waterway for trade, transport and amusement, as well as being a source of fresh fish. Try not to fall in: the current is very strong and help may not be readily to hand to fish you out.

... and Hills

There is high ground overlooking the Tiber at this spot. The Palatine, Capitoline and Aventine are the most obvious of its legendary seven hills (see pages 28–9), but the modern city encompasses more than just the original seven. Indeed, the **Pincio** (Pincian hill, see page 119) and the **Gianicolo** (Janiculum hill), which provides Trastevere with its westernmost boundary, stand out more prominently, possibly because they have relatively few buildings. The Pincio is dominated by the Villa Medici (see page 111) and the Gianicolo by a tree-lined fringe running along its brow. The Vatican City is located on the flank of **Monte Vaticano**, while **Monte Testaccio**, south of the Aventine is a man-made 'hill' created by the dumping, from about 140BC to AD250, of millions of fragments of broken amphorae, used to carry goods to nearby warehouses.

Culture

*I*taly has an enormous cultural heritage. It is estimated that over two-thirds of the western world's great works of art are in Italy, and Rome is the proud minder of a substantial chunk of this heritage. Much of it relates to the history of the Catholic church, the seat of which, the Vatican City, lies in the very heart of the city and is a treasury of the visual arts.

Latter-day Patronage of the Arts

In Italy government funding for the arts is notoriously limited. Fortunately there is widespread and lavish sponsorship by big business with special exhibitions and projects funded by industrial giants. One example of this was the 1993 exhibition on the history of Pompeii at Rome's Museo Capitolino, which was financed by Olivetti, whose name was much to the fore on exhibition banners, catalogues and so on. The controversial cleaning of Michelangelo's ceiling frescos in the Cappella Sistina, was paid for by Nippon (see page 100), while Fiat donated a whole museum to Rome, the Museo della Civiltà Romana at EUR (see page 57).

Cultural Pastimes

Rome's opera, theatre and concerts are well attended. This is not necessarily a mark of the excellence of the productions (they are often undistinguished), but is more an illustration of the Romans' generally enthusiastic attitude to the arts. Cinema is a genuinely popular pastime for Romans.

Religion

Italy is the world's centre of Catholicism, Rome its heart. Yet the Romans are famously uninterested in religion, in spite of the fact that their city has the greatest number of religious buildings anywhere in the Christian world. Although they may be proud of the heritage these places represent, regular attendance at mass is on the decline among the Catholics of Rome. Few involve themselves in the religious life of their city except when there are saints' days to observe, and even then this is mainly because of their superstitious

Everywhere in Rome images from the past provide the backdrop to modern daily life

FIRST STEPS

If you are at Rome, live in the Roman style; if you are elsewhere, live as they live elsewhere.

JEREMY TAYLOR,
English Divine (1613–67)

ARRIVING

Rome has two main airports. **Leonardo da Vinci** (36km from Rome), also known as **Fiumicino**, is the bigger and is equipped with the kind of services you expect from an international airport: bureaux de change, post office, and so on. **Ciampino** (16km out of town) caters mostly for charter flights and does not even have a tourist information desk. Getting into town from the airports is fairly simple: there is a direct rail line from Leonardo da Vinci to the large and busy **Termini** railway station and another rail line stopping at several stations and linking with the Metro, while half-hourly buses run from Ciampino, with connections to Termini. For more details see page 178.

Dashing home for lunch

SOMEWHERE TO STAY

Rome is a popular holiday location, particularly for 'weekend breaks'. It gets very busy in the summer months and is full of visitors at Easter and Christmas. Ideally, you should book accommodation in advance, but if this is not possible Leonardo da Vinci airport, Termini railway station and the tourist office in Rome all have hotel reservations facilities.

Accommodation is varied, ranging from the opulent to the down-at-heel, from residential hotels to self-catering holiday apartments and hostels. Campsites are a fair distance from the heart of Rome and only advisable if daily visits to the city are not central to your Lazio itinerary. The most popular hotels are those overlooking some hallowed view, such as the Pantheon or Campo dei Fiori. If you like to throw open your window at sunrise and see something truly magical a stone's throw away, then book your accommodation at least two months before you go. See also pages 172–5.

THE LIE OF THE LAND

One way to get some idea of locations and distances is to head for the nearest vantage point – the Pincian, Aventine or Janiculum hills are the best – and try to pinpoint the landmarks with the help of a good map. Luckily the main landmarks can be seen from afar: look for the domes of key churches and the bulk of others like the Pantheon and the Colosseum which jut out way above their neighbours.

The historic centre of Rome is actually quite small and easy to comprehend. Briefly, the River Tiber divides the Vatican City to the northwest and the Trastevere district to the southwest from the city's ancient core. This, the *centro storico*, is located between the river and the seven hills to the east and southeast.

PLANNING YOUR DAY

It is a good idea to plan a timetable at the start of each day, paying special attention to the idiosyncratic opening times of the museums and galleries. Why waste time setting out in search of Caesar or the creative genius of Michelangelo only to discover on arrival that the venue is shut for lunch or has long been closed for restoration? Remember also that most places close for a long lunch, and reopen late in the afternoon.

GETTING AROUND

The best way to see Rome is on foot. Many of the sights are tightly packed at its centre, and walking between them increases the chance of stumbling unexpectedly on some little square or handsome doorway. It is also the best way to discover appealing cafés and bars or interesting shops.

As with many big cities, if you confine yourself to the public transport system you will never discover the real living city, which can only be found by getting out into the streets of Rome. If you get lost, don't worry. The Romans love to help and will helpfully direct – or misdirect – you.

Bus, Metro and taxi

For non-walkers a reasonably efficient bus service criss-crosses town, and the Metropolitana underground system is useful if you need to cross town quickly. Yellow metered taxis are omnipresent and are handy for visits to suburban sites. See also page 187.

Bridges over the River Tiber

Where to go next: taking a bearing

CENTRAL ROME

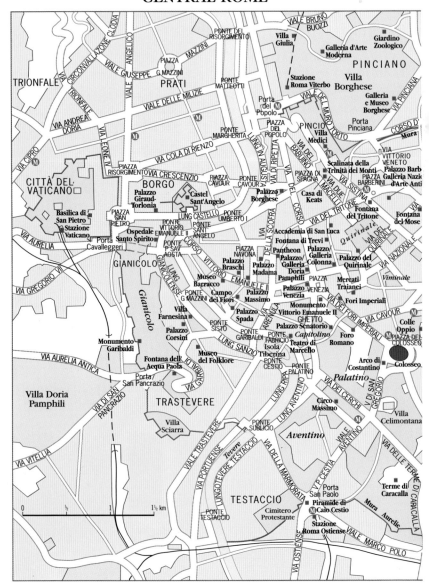

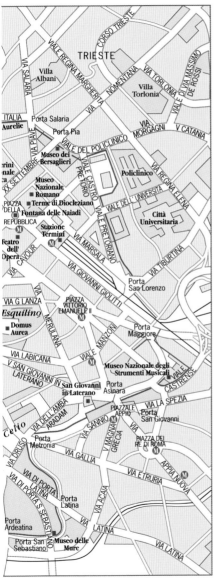

Save your legs

Bicycles, Vespas and mopeds can all be rented in the city. The last two modes of transport are another good way of getting to outlying sites provided you are undeterred by the mad, unpredictable antics of the local traffic. Cycling should not be attempted by the faint-hearted: bikes and Roman car drivers are not always compatible, particularly so during the mayhem of rush hour.

SIGHTSEEING TOURS

The local bus company and certain private companies organise tours of Rome (see page 188). Private guides are also available at a price – consult the tourist office.

❖

THOMAS COOK'S
Rome

*When Thomas Cook began his
European tours, the capital of the
Kingdom of Italy was Turin.
Rome was not included in Cook's first trip
to Italy in the summer of 1864 but he
advised that those wishing to visit it were
at liberty to do so, and could rejoin
the main party later. By 1866 Cook was
organising a special trip to Rome for Easter,
taking in Paris, Turin, Florence, Pisa,
Leghorn and Milan en route, for a first class
fare of £20.00. It was at this time that
Cook began negotiating with hotel
proprietors for reasonable rates.
The first Cook's office in Rome opened at
504 The Corso in 1874.*

A seat in the shade at the Palazzo Farnese

DOING IT THEIR WAY: CUSTOMS, MORES, MANNERS

How do you address an attractive stranger you would like to get to know without being over-familiar? Are those two men walking by arm-in-arm gay, or just good friends? How do you handle the gropers? Social mores in Italy, as everywhere, are a minefield of subtle nuances heavy with meaning. It is easy to offend or to send out the wrong message. Described below are some of things you should be aware of.

Greetings

It is not uncommon for two men to greet each other, or bid each other farewell, with a kiss on each cheek. Nothing more than a conventional sign of affection, it is a social ritual which women and couples also indulge in. The kiss, *un bacio*, comes in varying degrees of fervour, from a wet squelch planted firmly mid-cheek, to a bumping of cheeks, to a mere kissing of air somewhere in the region of your partner's face. Whichever, it signals that you are more than just acquaintances. More formally, shake hands on meeting and say *piacere* (pleased to meet you). Subsequently, you might say *buon giorno* (good morning) or *buona sera* (good afternoon), followed by *arrivederci* (goodbye). Informally, among friends, just say *ciao* on every occasion (though to

The vegetable sellers at Campo dei Fiore

an older person this might be considered rude). There are degrees of formality which vary from generation to generation, but these are very basic rules and nobody will mind if you get them wrong.

Handling unwanted admirers
If you are female and alone and are being irritated by the over-persistent attentions of Roman admirers, the best advice is to ignore them. Look bored or scornful; never do anything that might be considered a come-on, which will only encourage them to crowd in on you. If all else fails, deliver a sound slap to the cheek.

On the phone
There are various ways to answer the phone in Italy. A hotel receptionist will probably give the name of the hotel first, but if you call a shop, business or the post office, the receptionist might just say *Dica* (which, roughly translated, means 'yes, speak!') or *Si?* (yes?). A better trained receptionist would say *Pronto* (hello). *Pronto* is generally used in a social context at home, though *Dica* and *Si?* are also common – as is *Chi è* (who is it?).

Sartorial advice
If you wear something odd or outrageous, expect to be laughed at or stared at – most Italians are deeply conventional. Although life in Rome is fairly casual, Italians on the whole like to look smart. Be warned: it can be daunting when the assistants in chic boutiques stare at your comfortable but shapeless holiday-wear. Churches have a strict dress code which must be followed: no shorts, mini-skirts,

vests or revealing tops. Do not even think of going barefoot.

Some do's and don't's
Italians sometimes have an easier attitude to what might be considered horrendous *faux pas* elsewhere, but it is worth bearing the following points in mind.
• Never get drunk in public. Although wine flows freely and lavishly at lunch and dinner, you rarely see an Italian incapable through drink. In fact this is frowned upon, particularly in public places.
• Italians are a nation of smokers. To light up in the middle of a meal is perfectly acceptable in Italy.
• Italian women do not expect a man to stand up when they enter the room, but they are delighted – and amused – when he does.
• It will not be appreciated if you wander around a church during mass (unless the building is big enough for you not to be noticed).

A lone prayer in the quiet

THE SEVEN HILLS

Every visitor knows of the seven hills on which Rome was built. Their very names – Aventino (Aventine), Capitolino (Capitoline), Celio (Celian), Esquilino (Esquiline), Palatino (Palatine), Quirinale (Quirinal) and Viminale (Viminal) – are resonant with history.

PALATINO

Legend has it that, in 753BC, the twins Romulus and Remus asked the gods which of them should rule their Tiber-side settlement. While Remus climbed the Aventine to await an omen, Romulus went up the Palatine. When six vultures flew over the Aventine and 12 over the Palatine, each thought he had been favoured. Romulus began building his city and, when his furious brother jumped over the walls, killed him. Romulus' settlement grew and prospered and, in time, the Palatine came to be covered with magnificent imperial palaces and gardens. Some evocation of their beauty lingers on today in the Orti Farnesiani from whose terraces are some of the loveliest views of Rome.

AVENTINO

The ancient Temple of Diana (patroness of wild things and of women), traditionally built by King Servius Tullius, and

the Temple of Juno Regina (wife and sister of Jupiter and one of Rome's principal goddesses – of women and marriage) once stood on the Aventine. Mark Antony's home was here too (though he spent much of the last years of his life in Egypt with Cleopatra). Today Santa Sabina (see page 121) is the Aventine's most hallowed spot.

QUIRINALE, VIMINALE AND ESQUILINO

These three hills rise to a plateau which, near the Porta Pia (see page 70), reaches 63m. On the Quirinal the Palazzo del Quirinale (see page 67) replaces the Temple of Quirinus (293BC), where Romulus was worshipped as Mars, god of war. To the east are the Viminal, brought into Rome's orbit by Servius Tullius whose wall encompassed it, and the Esquiline with its two summits, the *Cispius* and the *Oppius*. The *Cispius* is topped by Santa Maria Maggiore, latest in a long line of places of worship sited here (see page 84), and on the *Oppius* are the ruins of the Domus Aurea (Nero's Golden House) and of the Terme di Traiano (Baths of Trajan).

CAPITOLINO

This, the smallest of the hills, is also the most famous. It has two ridges, the *Arx* and the *Capitolium*. The ancient fortress Citadel and the Temple of Juno Moneta (replaced by Santa Maria in Aracoeli – see page 82) crowned the *Arx*. On the *Capitolium* stood the Capitol, ancient Rome's principal temple, dedicated to Jupiter. Today the hill is dominated by Michelangelo's Piazza del Campidoglio (see page 68) containing Palazzo Senatorio, Rome's town hall, and the Museo Capitolino (see page 56).

CELIO

The magnificent gardens of Nero's Domus Aurea (Golden House) once adorned the Celian, but by the 16th century it was covered with woods, the haunt of wild boar and deer. Today the hill is the site of a large, peaceful park surrounded by some of Rome's most ancient churches.

Far left: the Palatine
Above: the Capitoline (left) and Santa Maria Maggiore, on the Esquiline (right).
Left: the wolf suckles Romulus and Remus

Above: the Piazza San Pietro is dominated by both the basilica and the palace
Left: the piazza seen from the roof of the Basilica San Pietro

buildings which incorporate columns, capitals and other bits of ancient Rome, reused by builders who simply took what was easiest to hand. Many churches and other buildings were in fact built on the sites of ancient Roman structures. On the edge of the *centro storico*, between the Palatine, Capitoline and the lower slopes of the Esquiline hills, lie the ruins of the ancient Forum. Just beyond is the Colosseum.

The **Vatican City**, out on a limb north of the Tiber, deserves an entire day's visit. There is much to see here, most notably St Peter's basilica, which is huge, the vast museums and the Sistine Chapel, entered via the museums. In the neighbourhood near the museum entrance there are many little cafés and other places to eat. Facing St Peter's is the Borgo district, famous for its forbidding castle, Castel Sant'Angelo.

Just to the south, still on the west bank of the Tiber, **Trastevere** also has some wonderful sights: spend a day or two here and imbibe its character. They say that the inhabitants of Trastevere are the true descendants of the ancient Romans. Visit their churches in the morning and afternoon, and lunch in a local *trattoria* in between.

WHAT IS WHERE

There are four main what might be termed 'visitor zones': the *centro storico* (historic centre), lying between the city's seven hills and the Tiber, roughly the area south and north of the Corso Vittorio Emanuele as far as the foot of the Spanish Steps; the hills themselves; the Vatican City; and the district of Trastevere. Further afield are the catacombs and some of Rome's earliest basilicas, each of which will require a special trip.

By far the greatest concentration of sights is in the **centro storico** and on the **seven hills**. In among the narrow streets and *piazze* of the former, are the Renaissance and baroque churches, the baroque squares and most of the fountains. Here it is not unusual to find

WHAT TO SEE

In truth Rome was greater, and
greater are its ruins than I imagined.
I no longer wonder that the whole
world was conquered by the city but
that I was conquered so late.

PETRARCH, (c. 1350)

THE BORGIAS

The rich Spanish Cardinal Borgia who became Pope Alexander VI in 1492 fathered at least six illegitimate sons and a beautiful daughter, Lucrezia, whose reputation has always been enigmatic. History still debates whether or not she was a willing conniver in murder, debauchery and incest or a long-suffering pawn in the political machinations of her father and ruthless brother, Cesare (who dealt with anyone who stood in his way by having him strangled in the dungeons of the Castel Sant'Angelo). The Borgias' activities caused the Dominican friar Savonarola to call Rome 'the sink of iniquity'. And yet, Alexander adorned the city with beautiful buildings and streets, and enhanced the Vatican Palace with a new set of apartments (see page 100).

The Aurelian Wall, the finest defence wall in the Roman Empire

ARA PACIS, see page 104.

AURELIE, MURA (Aurelian Walls)
Extensive sections of Rome's ancient walls, begun by Emperor Aurelian in AD271 to defend Rome against the barbarians, have survived. The walls remained the city's main defence until 1870 when they were finally breached at the Porta Pia (see page 70) by artillery of the united Italian army who subsequently took Rome.

Originally the wall was 19km long, its vast circuit encompassing all seven of Rome's hills. Built of brick, its ramparts were 3.6m thick and 6m high, with 18 gates surmounted by protective towers housing heavy artillery.

Also see the **Museo delle Mura** (page 57).

The most imposing surviving sections are: the buttressed portion on Via Campania east

of Porta Pinciana – buses to Via Vittorio Veneto 52, 53, 56, 58, 58b, 95, Metro Barberini; and sections surrounding Porta Asinaria (see page 70) – buses 4, 15, 16, 81, 85, 87, Metro San Giovanni. Of the gateways, Porta San Sebastiano (see page 71), which leads directly to Via Appia Antica (see page 116), is the most interesting – bus 118.

BORGO

Tight up against St Peter's and the Piazza San Pietro is the district known as the Borgo. Always an area of pilgrims' lodgings, monasteries and churches, today it is crowded with hotels, cafés and shops selling religious souvenirs. The Borgo was probably founded by the English King Ine of Wessex, who renounced his kingdom in 726 to spend his remaining days in Rome. He built a church for Saxon pilgrims on the site of the present-day church of **Santo Spirito in Sassia**. Attached to this is the 15th-century **Ospedale Santo Spirito**, originally a foundlings' home, later a hospice for pilgrims and still both an orphanage and hospital.

Much of the Borgo was devastated when the Via della Conciliazione was built in the 1930s as a grand approach to St Peter's. Originally the Borgo was defined by the **Leonine Walls** built by Pope Leo IV following the Saracen attack on St Peter's in 846. They ran from Castel Sant'Angelo to the foot of the hill behind St Peter's and back to the river beside the Ospedale. A good chunk of the wall survives north of Via della Conciliazione, including a section containing the so-called *passetto*, a small corridor linking the Vatican and Castel Sant'Angelo. It was used by Pope Alexander VI in 1494, to escape to the fortress during the invasion of Rome by

Charles VIII of France.

One of the Borgo's most splendid palaces is the **Palazzo Giraud-Torlonia**, built in the 15th century for Cardinal Adriano Castellesi da Corneto, papal nuncio in England and friend of the English king Henry VII. Until the Reformation it was the residence of Henry VIII's ambassadors to the Holy See.

Ospedale Santo Spirito, Borgo Santo Spirito 2. Chapel open daily, 8.30am–2pm. Buses to the Borgo: 23, 34, 41, 46, 64.
Palazzo Giraud-Torlonia, Via della Conciliazione 30. Not open to the public.

The Aurelian Wall originally protected an area much larger than the inhabited part of Rome

Castel Sant'Angelo

*B*uilt in AD139 as a mausoleum for Emperor Hadrian, this famous Rome landmark subsequently served as a fortress, prison and papal palace. In 1870 it became a barracks and military prison and was converted into a museum in 1933. The building's name derives from Pope Gregory the Great's vision during the plague of 590, when he saw an angel sheathing his sword on the castle's summit. Taking this as a sign that the plague was over, he built a chapel on the site of the vision and renamed the fortress. The 18th-century bronze Archangel Michael atop the Castel Sant'Angelo is a reminder of these events.

The Structure

The mausoleum was constructed alongside a pagan necropolis which would later contain the tomb of St Peter and other Christians. Originally it was a marble and travertine-clad drum topped by a tumulus of soil with a gilded statue of Hadrian as a charioteer at its pinnacle.

The drum survives as the core of the present structure.

The building consists of three basic interlinked elements: a battlemented exterior with Alexander VI's four corner bastions (it was fortified from the time of Aurelian onwards and was a mainstay of Rome's defences in the Middle Ages); the original tomb at its core; and a square tower, also partly original, above the latter. Other buildings were constructed against and over the tower from the 15th century onwards.

What to See

There is much to see spread out over four levels. Entry is via Hadrian's tomb, and a shallow ramp spirals up to his funerary chamber, the Sala del Tesoro (Treasury). The magnificent marbles with which it was decorated have vanished, though the lid of his sarcophagus survives as a baptismal font in St Peter's. At the base of the building is the Chamber of the Urns, which housed the imperial ashes placed in the wall recesses. Near by is the 15th-century San Marocco prison where important prisoners (Benvenuto Cellini and Cesare Borgia among them) were held in gruesome conditions.

The Archangel Michael sheaths his sword

The Castel Sant'Angelo has served as fortress, prison and palace

On the second level lies the Cortile di Onore (Courtyard of Honour) with its piles of cannon-balls, Raffaello da Montelupo's 16th-century marble angel (originally on top of the castle) and a chapel with a façade designed by Michelangelo. Opening from the courtyard is a warren of corridors and apartments built and decorated for various popes. Look out for Clement VII's bathroom with its grotesques by Giulio Romano, and the apartments commissioned by Paul III. These include the Sala di Apollo (Hall of Apollo), decorated by pupils of Perino del Vaga and, in the little room beyond, Luca Signorelli's *Madonna and Saints* and a triptych by Taddeo Gaddi. The Sala della Giustizia (Hall of Justice) contains Perino del Vaga's magnificent *Angel of Justice*. Also on this level lies the Cortile di Alessandro VI (Courtyard of

Alexander VI) with a wellhead carrying the Borgia coat of arms.

On the third floor is the Loggia of Paul III, designed by Antonio da Sangallo the Younger, and Bramante's Loggia for Julius II. Here, too, is the castle's most splendid room, the Sala Paolina, Paul III's council hall, decorated with frescos by del Vaga mostly representing episodes from the lives of Alexander the Great and St Paul (Pope Paul's real name was Alessandro – Alexander). There is a representation of Hadrian on the opposite wall. Beyond lies the Sala della Biblioteca (Hall of the Library), decorated in part with scenes from the life of Hadrian.

Lungotevere Castello (tel: 687 5036).
Open: winter, daily, 9.00am–1pm; summer, daily, 9am–7pm. Sunday, all year, 9.00am–1pm. Admission charge. Buses: 23, 34, 49, 64, 87, 280. Metro: Lepanto.

The Catacombs

*T*he catacombs, of which there are 67 known ones in Rome, are underground cemeteries, the Christian burial grounds of the first four centuries. Sanctuaries were later built near the crypts of the martyrs. Despite the Roman authorities' disapproval of the early Christians, their respect for the dead was too great to allow the catacombs to be damaged, and much has survived. Many galleries were rediscovered in the 19th century having been abandoned or forgotten, and in the 1840s Pope Gregory XVI took measures to preserve this evidence of early Christian history. The catacombs are important for their inscriptions, and they contain some of the earliest surviving examples of Christian art.

One good way to see and experience the catacombs, and to elicit an emotional response to hallowed surroundings of great antiquity, is to attend Mass in one or other of them.

CATACOMBE DI DOMITILLA
(Catacombs of Domitilla)

The Catacombs of Domitilla are notable for both their classical and Christian paintings, including the earliest known depiction of Christ as the Good Shepherd. They form one of the largest networks of underground burial sites in the city: on four levels, the catacombs have around

Dank and musty, the Catacombs of San Callisto are among the most ancient of Rome's burial grounds

DICKENS ON THE CATACOMBS

Charles Dickens, in *Pictures from Italy*, talks about the catacombs with their 'pictures, bad and wonderful, and impious, and ridiculous; of kneeling people, curling incense, tinkling bells, and sometimes (but not often) of a swelling organ; of Madonne, with their breasts stuck full of swords, arranged in a half-circle like a modern fan; of actual skeletons of dead saints hideously attired in gaudy satins, silks, and velvets trimmed with gold: their withered crust of skull adorned with precious jewels'.

17km of passages and crypts. They grew out of the early subterranean tomb of the family of Flavia Domitilla, a distant relative of Vespasian and Domitian. It is thought that Domitilla, with her servants Nereus and Achilleus, was exiled and later martyred for being Christian. According to Pope St Damasus I (*c*.304–*c*.384), Nereus and Achilleus were Roman soldiers who, on becoming Christian, refused to serve in the army and were put to death. More is known about them than of Domitilla, who is known to have been banished to the island of Pandateria around 96.

Not all the burial chambers here are Christian; many of those dating from the 1st and 2nd centuries are pagan. In the 4th century a basilica was built over the site though little remains of this apart from a bas-relief showing the martyrdom of St Achilleus. The present building is the result of much reconstruction in later periods.

Via delle Sette Chiese (tel:511 0342). Open: Wednesday to Monday, 8.30am–noon and 2.30pm–5pm. Closed January. Admission charge. Buses: 94, 218, 613.

CATACOMBE DI PRISCILLA (Catacombs of Priscilla)

These are based on the tomb of a Roman family, the Acilii, who in the 1st century AD owned much of the land in the vicinity, and one of whose members, Priscilla, was put to death on the orders of Domitian. Among Rome's oldest catacombs, they contain some of the finest early Christian paintings, including the earliest known depiction of the *Madonna and Child* as well as the first known representation of *The Breaking of the Bread at the Last Supper*, in what is known as the 'Greek Chapel'.

Via Salaria 430 (tel: 8380408). Open:

In the catacombs, neat shelves cut into the rock housed the dead

Tuesday to Sunday, 8.30am–noon and 2.30pm–5.00pm. Admission charge. Buses: 56, 57.

CATACOMBE DI SAN SEBASTIANO AND SAN CALLISTO (Catacombs of St Sebastian and St Calixtus), see page 116.

Gateway to the burial ground

Colosseo

(Colosseum)

*T*he ruins of this majestic building are one of the best known sights of Rome, though its present state belies its former magnificence. Originally the entire structure was lined with travertine, a local limestone, but over the centuries this was plundered for use elsewhere. What we see today is a handsome ruin – the preserve of feral cats and wild flowers – bounded by a hefty curtain wall in four tiers and with a large pit at its centre.

There were 80 arched entrances to the building: 76 for the public, two for the Emperor's entourage and two for the gladiators. Of the latter, one was for those who managed to survive to return to their quarters, while the other – named after Libitina, goddess of death – was used for the removal of the corpses of the defeated. Inside were three main areas: the pit, the arena and the auditorium. Oval in plan, the 'pit' was once covered by the floor of the arena and is all that remains of the building's labyrinthine undercroft in which the wild animals and prisoners were housed.

The Arena

Built by Emperor Vespasian in AD72, on the site of a drained lake in the grounds

Inside the Colosseum

THE COLOSSEUM PLUNDERED
'This amphitheatre…might have stood entire for two thousand years to come: For what are the slow corrosions of time, in comparison of the rapid destruction from the fury of the Barbarians…and the avarice of Popes and Cardinals?' wrote Dr John Moore in the 18th century. The buildings constructed since the Renaissance from Colosseum stone include Palazzo Venezia, Palazzo Cancelleria, Palazzo Farnese and Villa Farnesina. The quarrying stopped in 1744 by order of Pope Benedict XIV, who placed a cross at the centre of the arena in memory of the martyrs who died there.

The Colosseum is Rome's most celebrated ancient monument

of Nero's palace, the Colosseum could hold 55,000 spectators and was the scene of the Roman Games and gladiatorial combats. The arena was extremely versatile: for animal combats it was planted with trees and scattered with rocks, and for the *naumachiae* it could be flooded to create a 'sea' on which battles between opposing 'navies' could be held. Realism was such that, if a scene in a play called for, say, the burning of Hercules on a funeral pyre, a convict played the part and was burnt alive. Cruelty was the regular fare: in the reign of Titus, nearly 5,000 animals were slaughtered in the arena.

The Auditorium

Surrounding the arena, the auditorium rose in tiers up to the highest point of the outer wall, 56m above the ground. The top floor was an enclosed colonnaded gallery for the women and the poor who sat on wooden seats. Immediately below this was a floor for slaves and foreigners. Further down were tiers of marble seats, the higher ones for the middle class, the lower ones for the more distinguished citizens. Just below this, more or less level with the ringside, were the seats and boxes for the senators, magistrates, priests, Vestal Virgins and members of the Emperor's family. In wet or very hot weather, sailors posted high on the roof would pull across the auditorium a coloured awning called the *velarium*. This was supported on poles fixed to the attic storey of the building and anchored on bollards outside it.

Piazza del Colosseo (tel: 700 4261). Open: times vary from 9am–7pm in summer to 9am–3pm in winter. Admission charge for upper tier only. Bus: 11 27, 81, 85, 87. Metro: Colosseo.

Palazzo dei Congressi, in the Esposizione Universale di Roma (EUR)

CORSO

The Via del Corso is one of the most dramatic streets in Rome. It cuts right through the city's heart from Piazza del Popolo to Piazza Venezia, following the line of the ancient Via Flaminia which led north from the Roman Forum. Today it is a buzzing shopping street where, at dusk, Romans strut and stroll.

At the Piazza Venezia end, the street was once called Via Lata and this was where Pope Paul II brought the Roman Carnival races (*corse*, hence Corso) in the 15th century. Races were held between Jews, old men, children, asses, buffaloes or riderless Arab horses made wild by nail-encrusted saddles. The crowds, 'swarming with whores, buffoons and all matter of rabble' (John Evelyn, 1645) and dressed as nymphs and gods, heroes and fairies, paraded up and down beneath buildings hung with foliage and ribbons. The races were discontinued at the end of the 19th century.

ROME AND THE FASCISTS

During the Fascist period, Rome was gradually transformed under the personal direction of Benito Mussolini. He announced to the City Council: 'In five years, Rome must tappear wonderful to the whole world, immense, orderly and powerful as she was in the days of the first empire of Augustus ... The Third Rome will extend over other hills ... as far as the shores of the Tyrrhenian Sea.' The huge EUR complex survives as an example of the grand scale of Fascist planning.

DOMINE QUO VADIS

This chapel, on Via Appia Antica (see page 116), commemorates the spot where St Peter is said to have met Christ while fleeing Rome after his escape from

the Mamertine Prison during Nero's persecution. After asking Christ, 'Domine quo vadis?' ('My Lord, where are you going?') and receiving the reply: 'I am going to Rome to be crucified for the second time', Peter took the hint and returned to his captors. According to tradition he was martyred by crucifixion – upside down. In the church you can see a replica of a stone allegedly containing Christ's footprint (the original is in San Sebastiano, see page 117).
Via Appia Antica. Buses: 118, 218.

EUR (ESPOSIZIONE UNIVERSALE DI ROMA)

About 5km south of central Rome is an area of interest to fans of Fascist architecture and town planning, the vast

Looking south down the Corso from Piazza del Popolo

Christ's footprints? Or a pagan offering after a safe journey?

1930s complex called EUR (Esposizione Universale di Roma). Its construction was part of Mussolini's grand design that envisaged a Rome vastly increased in size and population and dominated by enormous buildings and skyscrapers.

EUR's realisation, along with the construction of the Via dei Fori Imperiali and the Via della Conciliazione, were the only elements of the grandiose design to be carried out. With later additions EUR covers over 400 hectares. Other far more damaging projects, such as the avenue intended to link the Pantheon with Piazza Colonna, were mercifully never carried out.

EUR was to be the location for a proposed exhibition to celebrate the 20th anniversary of the Fascists' march on Rome . It was to be called 'The Olympics of Civilisation' and was to open in 1942 (its nickname was 'E42'). Work began in 1938 and by the outbreak of war, the church and the Palazzo della Civiltà del Lavoro, the so-called 'Square Colosseum', had been built. After the war, during which various occupying armies and then scores of refugees severely damaged the complex, work was continued and important additions include Nervi's Palazzo dello Sport (1958), used in the 1960s Olympics, and the vast Museo della Civiltà Romana (see page 57) which was presented to Rome by FIAT.
Bus: 93, 97, 197, 293, 493, 765. Metro: EUR Palasport, EUR Fermi.

Fontane

(Fountains)

FONTANA DELLE API, see page 119.

FONTANA DELL'ACQUA PAOLA, see page 115.

FONTANA DELLA BARCACCIA (Barcaccia Fountain)

Constructed in 1627–9 by Pope Urban VIII to bring water to the area between Piazza di Spagna and Porta del Popolo, the Barcaccia ('Worthless Boat') flows slowly because of low water pressure. The ingenious design, which may be by

Gian Lorenzo Bernini or possibly his father Pietro, represents a sinking leaky boat and was suggested by ancient Roman models.
Piazza di Spagna. Bus: 119. Metro: Spagna.

> *I like this city. It is full of the sound of water, fountains everywhere, amazing and beautiful – big things full of marble – gods and animals, naked girls wrestling with horses and swans with tons of water cascading over them.*
> William Faulkner (1954)

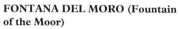

The massive figure of Neptune dominates the Trevi Fountain

FONTANA DEL MORO (Fountain of the Moor)

In Piazza Navona (south), this fountain, originally designed by Giacomo della Porta (1575), was rearranged by Bernini who made the figure of the Moor struggling with a dolphin.
Piazza Navona. Bus: 46, 62, 64, 70, 81, 87, 90.

FONTANA DEL MOSE (Fountain of Moses)

Also known as Fontana dell'Acqua Felice (Fountain of the 'Happy' Water), the fountain was built in 1585–7 by Domenico Fontana for Pope Sixtus V, whose original Christian name was Felice. In addition to the central figure of Moses, side relief panels depict Aaron, Joshua and the Israelites.
Piazza S Bernardo. Bus: 60, 61, 62, 65, 492. Metro: Repubblica.

FONTANA DELLE NAIADI
(Fountain of the Naiads)

This huge fountain shocked Rome when it was unveiled in 1901 to reveal its four groups of bronze Naiads (river nymphs) frolicking nude astride aquatic beasts. Try to see it floodlit.

Piazza della Repubblica. Bus: 4, 16, 36, 38, 60, 61, 62, 65, 75. Metro: Repubblica.

FONTANA DEI QUATTRO FIUMI
(Fountain of the Four Rivers)

The fountain was completed in 1651 for the Pamphili pope Innocent X. Centrepiece of the Piazza Navona, it is one of Bernini's greatest triumphs. The figures personify the four great rivers of the world: Danube, Ganges, River Plate (whose raised hand is said to be 'preventing' Borromini's Sant'Agnese from falling – a jibe aimed at Bernini's rival) and Nile (covering its eyes – possibly an allusion to its then unknown source). In the middle, surmounted by the Pamphili armorial dove, rises a Roman obelisk removed from the Circus of Maxentius (see page 117).

Piazza Navona. Bus: see Fontana del Moro above.

FONTANA DELLE TARTARUGHE
(Fountain of the Tortoises)

Designed in 1585 by Giacomo della Porta, this is one of the most elegant fountains in Rome. The detailing is the work of the Florentine, Taddeo Landini: four bronze youths balance on the heads of dolphins while supporting tortoises (17th-century additions by Bernini).

Piazza Mattei. Bus: 44, 56, 60, 65, 75, 170.

FONTANA DI TREVI (Trevi Fountain)

The most famous of Rome's fountains is

Succour for tired feet: the cool waters of the Trevi Fountain provide welcome relief for the weary

the work of Niçolò Salvi who started it in 1732, more than a century after the project was abandoned by Bernini, and was completed by Gianpaolo Pannini in 1762. Its name is thought to derive from the *tre vie* (three roads) which converge here, and it is the fountainhead of the Acqua Vergine aqueduct which has brought water to this site since 19BC. Neptune, at the centre, is flanked by Tritons, one struggling to control his horse, symbolising stormy seas, while his conch-blowing companion represents the ocean in repose. In the niches on either side of Neptune are Health and Abundance and above are the Four Seasons. People throw coins over their shoulder into the fountain to ensure a speedy return to Rome.

Piazza Fontana di Trevi. Bus: 52, 53, 58, 60, 61, 62, 71.

FONTANA DEL TRITONE, see page 119.

Forums

*T*he Foro Romano (Roman Forum) was an early market place whose name derives from its location 'outside the walls' (the original meaning of *forum*). It became the centre of the political, commercial and judicial life of Rome, and over the centuries emperors embellished it with magnificent temples and basilicas. As Rome grew and the original Forum became too small, Julius Caesar and his successors from Augustus to Trajan built new ones. Some of these so-called Imperial Forums lie partially buried beneath Mussolini's Via dei Fori Imperiali, still unexcavated and unexplored. Ironically, more survives of the old original Forum than from any of the newer ones.

FORO ROMANO (Roman Forum)
After entering you come first to the **Tempio di Antonio e Faustina**, built by Emperor Antoninus Pius in AD141 to honour his wife, Faustina. It was converted into a church (San Lorenzo in Miranda) in the 11th century because it was thought that St Lawrence was condemned to death here. The nearby **Via Sacra**, Rome's most ancient street, runs through the Forum and was the scene of the victorious return of campaigning armies. Built in 179BC by Marcus Aemilius Lepidus, the **Basilica Aemilia** (a business centre and money exchange) was ruined by Alaric in AD410.

ROMAN FORUM

The Roman Forum is a reminder of the might of ancient Rome

The once marble-clad **Curia** beyond, the seat of the Roman senate, goes back to 80BC; its original doors can be seen at San Giovanni in Laterano (page 78).

The **Arco di Settimo Severo** was erected in AD203 to celebrate the 10th anniversary of the accession of Septimius Severus. Below the arch is the **Imperial Rostra**, the public speaking platform placed here by Caesar and decorated with captured ships' prows (*rostra*). According to Shakespeare, it was from here that Mark Antony delivered his 'Friends, Romans, countrymen' speech. The **Colonna di Foca** (Column of Phocas), before the Rostra, was erected in honour of Emperor Phocas who gave the Pantheon to Pope Boniface IV (608).

All that remains of the **Tempio di Vespasiano** (Vespasian's temple – AD79) are three fluted columns, for centuries lone symbols of the buried Forum's lost grandeur. Eight columns survive of the **Tempio di Saturno**, dedicated to Saturn, god of agriculture, in whose honour the December festivities of feasting and sacrificing – the *Saturnalia* – were held.

Erected by Julius Caesar in 54BC (re-built AD304), the huge **Basilica Giulia** was a courthouse and meeting place of the four civic tribunals. The **Tempio di Castore e Polluce** next door, dedicated to the mythical twins, Castor and Pollux, was rebuilt by Tiberius (*c*.AD12).

The circular **Tempio di Vesta** (4th-century AD) housed the 'eternal flame', symbol of Rome's continuity. It was guarded by the Vestal Virgins, who lived in the neighbouring **Atrium Vestae**.

With porphyry columns and bronze doors, the **Tempio di Romolo** is thought to have been built in AD309 by Maxentius in honour of his dead son Romulus. The vast **Basilica di Maxentius** for administering justice and for the conduct of business was built in AD306.

Beyond, and abutting Santa Francesca Romana, the huge **Tempio di Venere e Roma** was erected by Hadrian in AD135 in the atrium of the Domus Aurea, Nero's Golden House. The great **Arco di Tito** not far away, built by Domitian in AD81 in honour of his brother Titus, is Rome's oldest triumphal arch.

DI CESARE (Caesar's Forum)

Julius Caesar's was the earliest of the Imperial Forums, built (54–46BC) with booty from wars waged in Gaul. Its principal buildings were the Temple of Venus Genetrix and a colonnade containing a row of shops which burned down in AD80. Domitian and Trajan rebuilt the colonnade and also constructed the Basilica Argentaria for moneychangers. Not much survives above ground apart from three columns. *Via del Carcere Tulliano (tel: 671 03065). Open by appointment only.*

Augustus's Forum

FORO DI AUGUSTO (Forum of Augustus)

During his reign Emperor Augustus inaugurated an ambitious building programme, transforming Rome 'from a city of brick into one of marble', as he himself put it. With the possible help of Greek architects, he constructed a new forum north of and at right angles to Julius Caesar's. Two sides of it were lined with immense colonnades, and its focus was a white marble temple. Completed in 2BC, the temple was filled with treasures and dedicated to Mars Ultor (Mars the Avenger) in commemoration of Augustus' victory at Philippi (42BC), where retribu-tion for Caesar's murder was exacted. A high wall, which still exists at the rear of the Forum, separated it from the poor, densely populated Subura district which lay between the Esquiline and Viminal hills. Little else survives here other than three of the temple's columns and, to the west of the Forum, the Medieval Casa dei Cavalieri di Rodi (House of the Knights of Rhodes) where the atrium is all that remains of the Augustan palace.
Piazza del Grillo 1 (tel: 671 02475). Open by appointment only.

FORO DI VESPASIANO (Vespasian's Forum)

Built between AD 71 and 75 by the emperor who began the Colosseum (see page 38), Vespasian's Forum is, like the other Imperial Forums, now partly obscured by the Via dei Fori Imperiali. In AD68 the Jews had rebelled against the Romans and the bitter war that ensued led to the fall of Jerusalem and the Jewish Diaspora. Vespasian used the spoils of the Temple of Jerusalem to construct a huge colonnaded area north-west of the present church of SS Cosma e

> *The intoxification [of ruins], at once so heady and so devout, is not the romantic melancholy engendered by broken towers and mouldered stones; it is the soaring of the imagination … it is the stunning impact of world history on its amazed heirs.*
> ROSE MACAULAY,
> *The Pleasure of Ruins (1953)*

Three forlorn columns of the Roman Forum's Temple di Vespasiano

Damiano (which stands on the site of the forum's library). It contained the Temple of Peace, dedicated in AD75, which according to Pliny was one of the principal sights of Rome.

South of the Via dei Fori Imperiali. Buses: 11, 27, 81, 85, 87, 186.

FORO DI NERVA (Nerva's Forum)

Nerva's Forum (AD96–8) is represented by two columns – the last remains of a colonnade that once flanked the forum – supporting a frieze that depicts, in relief, the goddess Minerva and a group of women doing their household chores (Minerva was their patroness), along with a ruined podium belonging to the Temple of Minerva. The temple was plundered by Pope Paul V in 1606 to provide the stone for his Fontana dell'Acqua Paola (see page 115). Also called the Forum Transitorium, because it joined Vespasian's Forum of Peace with the Forum of Augustus, Nerva's Forum was constructed over the Argiletum, an ancient street leading into the Subura. Remains of the Argiletum can be seen at the foot of the two columns, the gulleys in its surface the result of years of wear by wagon wheels.

Piazza del Grillo 1 (via the Forum of Augustus). Closed for excavations.

A column in Augustus's Forum

PATRONAGE

In Rome's past, patronage of the arts was mainly the preserve of wealthy scholars, connoisseurs and popes. Artists were commissioned to embellish private chapels within churches to glorify a prominent person or family. Works were also commissioned to adorn the walls of private galleries, often as a symbol of a family's importance, for example Galleria Doria Pamphili, Galleria Colonna and Museo Borghese.

In the 16th century Popes Julius II and Leo X, the greatest patrons of the period, employed the greatest artists of the day, Michelangelo and Raphael, to adorn St Peter's. But no period in Rome's artistic history was more important for informed and cultivated patronage of the visual arts than the baroque in the 17th century.

During the baroque period the principal patrons were the popes, their nephews and their entourages who poured into Rome from all over Italy in search of lucrative posts in the government. Their increasing monopoly of wealth and power enabled them to dictate fashion. Paul V and Gregory XV set the pattern followed by Urban VIII, under whose pontificate St Peter's was completed. Each built and decorated a vast family palace and villa, established a luxurious family chapel in one of the city's important churches and supported and enriched religious foundations, while a favoured nephew set up his private gallery of pictures and sculpture (eg **Galleria Borghese**, page 50).

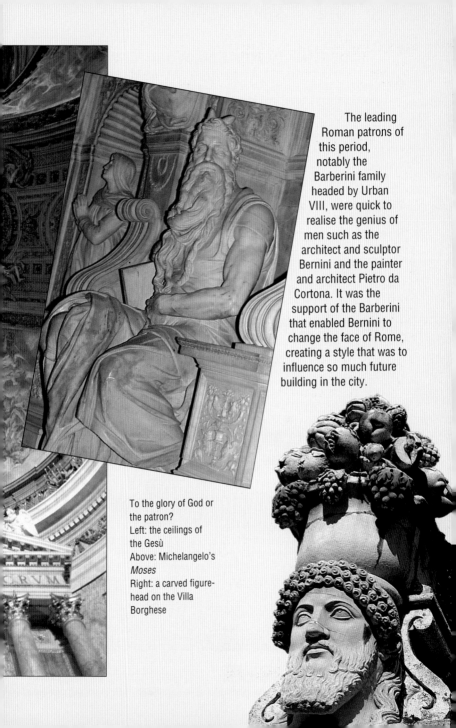

The leading Roman patrons of this period, notably the Barberini family headed by Urban VIII, were quick to realise the genius of men such as the architect and sculptor Bernini and the painter and architect Pietro da Cortona. It was the support of the Barberini that enabled Bernini to change the face of Rome, creating a style that was to influence so much future building in the city.

To the glory of God or the patron?
Left: the ceilings of the Gesù
Above: Michelangelo's *Moses*
Right: a carved figure-head on the Villa Borghese

CANOVA'S *PAULINE BORGHESE*

Canova at first wanted to represent Pauline as Diana the Huntress, but when she learned that Diana had asked her father to endow her with eternal virginity, Pauline refused. Eventually she was portrayed as Venus reclining nude on a couch, partially covered by a thin veil and with her right hand concealing her ear, her one imperfection. Originally Pauline was to have sat for the face alone, but when Canova expressed doubts about finding a model sufficiently beautiful to pose for the body, Pauline insisted that she pose herself. 'But why not?' she said, 'There was a good fire in the studio.'

GALLERIA D'ARTE MODERNA (Gallery of Modern Art)

This is Rome's main collection of art from 1800 onwards. Of its 20th-century Italian works, the most interesting are by the Futurists Umberto Boccioni and Giorgio de Chirico. Other artists represented in the gallery include Degas, Cézanne, Kandinsky, Max Ernst, Jackson Pollock and Henry Moore. *Viale delle Belle Arti 131 (tel: 322 4152). Open: summer, Tuesday to Saturday, 9am–7pm; Sunday and public holidays, 9am–1pm; rest of year, Tuesday to Saturday, 9am–2pm; Sunday, 9am–1pm. Admission charge. Tram: 19, 19b.*

GALLERIA E MUSEO BORGHESE (Borghese Gallery and Museum)

The gallery is a magnificent repository of art, particularly of the classical and baroque periods. The opulent lower floor (the *museo*) houses the sculpture, with the paintings on the upper floor (the *galleria*).

The gallery is housed in the summerhouse, or *casino*, of the Villa Borghese, built by Cardinal Scipione Borghese, a man 'devoted to the cultivation of pleasures and pastimes' as the Venetian ambassador of the day described him. The nephew of Pope Paul V, he pursued his love of art ruthlessly, even stealing paintings that he coveted: he had Raphael's *Deposition* removed from the Baglioni family chapel in Perugia at dead of night.

In the Museo Borghese, Bernini's *David* is about to kill Goliath

Above: *Pauline Borghese* by Canova, Galleria Borghese. Left: *Pope Innocent* by Velasquez, Galleria Colonna

He was one of the greatest patrons and collectors of his day and much of what is now in the gallery was his – although many of his pictures and sculptures were sold off before the state purchased the collection from his descendants in 1902. The exhibits include the famous family collection brought here from the Palazzo Borghese (see page 66) in 1891. Among the paintings you can still see Raphael's *Deposition*, and there is a whole room of Caravaggios, as well as works by Rubens, Bassano, Dossi, Titian, Antonello da Messina, Pinturicchio and Domenichino.

The collection's Bernini sculptures, notably the *Rape of Proserpine* (1621–2) and *Apollo and Daphne* (1622–5), are unrivalled. Here, too, is Canova's erotic statue of *Pauline Borghese* (1804 – see box). *Villa Borghese (tel: 854 8577). Open: Tuesday to Saturday, 9am–7pm (October to April: 2pm); Sunday, 9am–1pm. The ticket office closes ½ an hour before closing time. Admission charge. Bus: 52, 53, 910 (to Via Pinciana), 3, 4, 57 (to Via Po).*

GALLERIA COLONNA
(Colonna Gallery)

The privately owned 15th-century palace of the Colonnas, home of one of Rome's old patrician families, is the setting for this collection of paintings and antique sculpture. Here you can see paintings by Rubens, Tintoretto, Van Dyck, Veronese, Bronzino, Gaspard Dughet and Annibale Carracci, in addition to family portraits including one of Vittoria Colonna, the friend of Michelangelo. A vast salon, with ceiling frescos celebrating Marcantonio Colonna's victory over the Turks at the battle of Lepanto (1571), contains the bulk of the collection established by Cardinal Girolamo Colonna in the 17th century. *Via della Pilotta 17 (tel: 679 4362). Open: Saturday only, 9am–12.30pm. Closed August. Admission charge. Bus: 57, 64, 65, 70, 75, 81, 170.*

The Hall of Mirrors in the Galleria Doria Pamphilj is a sumptuous setting for the family treasures

marbles, baroque furniture and Gobelin tapestries.

Piazza del Collegio Romano 1A (tel: 679 4365). Open: Tuesday, Friday, Saturday and Sunday, 10am–1pm. Admission charge. Bus: 56, 60, 62, 85, 90, 95.

GALLERIA NAZIONALE D'ARTE ANTICA: PALAZZO BARBERINI E PALAZZO CORSINI (National Gallery of Early Art: Barberini Palace and Corsini Palace)

The **Palazzo Barberini** (1625–33) was built by Carlo Maderno with the help of Borromini and completed by Bernini for the powerful Barberini family. Part of the family collection is still housed here but this, along with the building and the rest of the contents, now belongs to the state. The palace's most important room is the Gran Salone whose centrepiece is Pietro da Cortona's ceiling painting *The Allegory of Divine Providence* (1638–9), which

GALLERIA DORIA PAMPHILI (Doria Pamphili Gallery)

The gallery is in the Palazzo Doria Pamphili, owned and still occupied by the Doria Pamphili family. The palace dates from 1435, though Valvassori's façade on the Via del Corso is early 18th century. A series of splendidly decorated state rooms, including a spectacular Hall of Mirrors, is open to the public .

Much of the collection was formed by Camillo Pamphili, nephew of Pope Innocent X whose portrait by Velasquez is here. The palace houses the contents of the Palazzo Pamphili (in Piazza Navona), which came to the Dorias through marriage. You can see Raphael's *Doppio Ritratto* (Double Portrait), important works by Bronzino, Caravaggio, Pietro da Cortona, Claude, Titian, Longhi and Bernini, and an excellent collection of ancient Roman

Palazzo Barberini once stood in a large park and was more country villa than town palace

celebrates the virtues of Pope Urban VIII for whom it was painted. Italian painting of the 13th to 16th centuries is well represented, with works by Fra Angelico, Perugino, Filippo Lippi, Lorenzo Lotto and Andrea del Sarto. Most famous of all is Raphael's *La Fornarina* (thought to be a portrait of his mistress). There are also works by Bronzino, Caravaggio and Canaletto and a portrait of England's King Henry VIII by Holbein.

The **Palazzo Corsini**, located across Rome in Trastevere, was originally built in the 15th century for Cardinal Riario and rebuilt in the 18th century for Cardinal Corsini by Ferdinando Fuga. The part of the National Gallery housed here includes paintings by Rubens, Murillo, Brueghel, Caravaggio and Guido Reni, together with a rare portrait of Bernini by Baciccia and 17th- and 18th-century regional Italian art.
Palazzo Barberini, Via delle Quattro Fontane 13 (tel: 481 4591). Open: Tuesday to Saturday, 9am–2pm; Sunday, 9am–1pm. Admission charge. Bus: 52, 53, 56, 58, 58b. Metro: Barberini.
Palazzo Corsini, Via della Lungara 10 (tel: 688 02323). Open: Tuesday to Saturday, 9am–2pm; Sunday and public holidays, 9am–1pm. Admission charge. Bus: 23, 41, 65.

GESÙ, see page 109.

GHETTO

Nowadays the old Jewish Ghetto is a charming area, but when it was established in 1555 Rome's Jews were suffering persecution. In 1556 Pope Paul IV erected a high wall around the area and the residents were locked in at night. Quaint now, it was once a dank, unhealthy place. In the past many

La Fornarina (the baker's daughter) by Raphael; supposedly a portrait of his mistress

sightseers came, including John Evelyn who in 1645 witnessed a circumcision, pronouncing it a 'slovenly ceremony'. On Sundays until 1848 the Jews were driven into Sant'Angelo in Pescheria to listen to sermons in the hope that they would convert to Christianity. In 1943 the Nazis occupied Rome and of the 2,000 Jews sent to concentration camps only 15 survived. The Synagogue (1848) is still in use.
Ghetto: Via Arenula – Teatro di Marcello, main street Via del Portico d'Ottavia. Synagogue at Lungotevere dei Cenci (telephone: 687 5051). Open: Monday to Thursday, 9.30am–2pm and 3pm–5pm; Friday, 9am–2pm; Sunday, 9am–12.30pm; closed Saturday. Bus: 23, 44, 56, 60, 65, 75.

ISOLA TIBERINA (Tiber Island)

Situated at a bend of the Tiber, Isola Tiberina is connected to the Ghetto (see page 53) by Ponte Fabricio (62BC), Rome's oldest surviving bridge, and to Trastevere by Ponte Cestio (46BC), rebuilt in the 19th century using original stone. To the south lie the remains of Pons Aemilius (179BC) – or Ponte Rotto (Broken Bridge) – Rome's first stone-arched bridge. The Romans also gave the boat-shaped southern point of the island a stone stern and prow and an obelisk for a mast.

The church of San Bartolomeo (see page 75) is on the site of a temple of Aesculapius, god of healing. According to legend one of the snakes of Aesculapius, being brought to Rome from Epidaurus during the plague of 293BC, escaped from the boat to this

> **AESCULAPIUS**
>
> The Greek god of healing, Aesculapius, died when Zeus struck him down with a thunderbolt for daring to bring the dead back to life. Snakes were sacred to Aesculapius, and when his cult was brought to Rome, the god himself was believed to have swum ashore in the form of a snake.

spot, which was taken as an omen that the god himself had chosen it. Today the Ospedale Fatebenefratelli ('hospital of the do-well brothers') on the island perpetuates the healing connection. *Bus: 15, 23, 97, 780.*

KEATS, CASA DI (KEATS-SHELLEY MEMORIAL MUSEUM)

In 1909 a museum was established in a house to the right of the Spanish Steps where, in 1821, the English poet John Keats died of consumption aged 25. The small room on the third floor is unchanged since his death. The little museum is filled with literary mementoes, drawings, photographs, prints and other assorted documents, along with Keats's life and death masks and locks of hair belonging to Keats, Shelley, John Milton and Elizabeth Barrett Browning .
Piazza di Spagna (tel: 678 4235). Open: Monday to Friday, 9am–1pm and 3–6pm (October to March: 2.30–5.30pm). Admission charge. Bus: 119. Metro: Spagna.

MERCATI TRAIANEI (Trajan's Market)

This well-preserved ancient 'shopping mall' with 150 outlets was built by Trajan in the 2nd century AD. It is

Hard by the Spanish Steps: the Keats-Shelley Memorial Museum

Trajan's Market was the 'shopping mall' of the ancients

spread over three levels of a series of semi-circular halls, two of which survive in excellent condition behind the Foro di Traiano. The products of the Empire's trade were sold here – silks, wine, oil, fruit, flowers and fish. Free corn was distributed to the poor in the *Congiara* at the top of the market.

The Via Biberatica (a medieval corruption of the Latin *pipera*, meaning pepper) was probably where the spice merchants congregated. The lower two storeys of the buildings lining the street appear much as they did in Trajan's time: the shop entrances with travertine surrounds – not unlike those in use in modern Rome – are cut into brick walls. Little wall openings above led to the mezzanine storage area.

Via 4 Novembre (telephone: 67 10 3613).
Open: Tuesday to Saturday, 9am–1.30pm;
Sunday, 9am–1pm; closed Monday. In summer (Apr–Sept) also open 9am–6pm on Thursday and Saturday. Admission charge. Bus: 57, 64, 65, 70, 75, 170.

MONUMENTO VITTORIO EMANUELE II (Victor Emanuel Monument)

This white Brescian marble monument (1911) to King Victor Emanuel II, first king of a unified Italy, sits on the north slope of the Capitoline. It contains a police station and the archives of the Istituto per la Storia del Risorgimento Italiano (Institute for the History of the Italian Risorgimento). On the terrace above the lower steps is the tomb of the Unknown Soldier, watched by a guard of honour.

Piazza Venezia. Not open to the public.
Bus: 56, 60, 64, 65, 70, 75.

At the Palazzo dei Conservatori of the Museo Capitolino a large antique foot dominates the courtyard

MUSEO CAPITOLINO (Capitoline Museum)

The world's first public museum, founded in the late 15th century, the Capitoline Museum's important collection is divided between two substantial buildings on the Piazza del Campidoglio.

The **Palazzo Nuovo** contains classical sculpture. Outstanding are the *Dying Gaul* (a Roman copy of a Greek 3rd-century BC bronze original), the *Discobolus* (a Greek discus thrower altered in the 18th century to create a wounded warrior) and the *Capitoline Venus* (copy of a 2nd-century BC Hellenistic original). The *Sala degli Imperatori* (Hall of the Emperors) takes its name from the busts of Roman emperors lining the walls; they once adorned the villas and gardens of ancient Rome.

The magnificent bronze equestrian statue (2nd century AD) of Marcus Aurelius, until recently outside in the piazza, is now inside the Palazzo Nuovo. Its original location was the piazza of the Lateran, often the scene of degradations inflicted on Roman citizens by the popes: in the 10th century Pope John XIII had the Prefect of Rome hung from the statue by his hair. Throughout the Middle Ages the figure on horseback was thought to represent Constantine, which may be the reason it was preserved, and by 1538 it was the

The Fascists commemorate the past: one exhibit in the fascinating Museo della Civiltà Romana

only monumental classical bronze to have survived. Much revered, it was removed to the Piazza del Campidoglio from which it was taken for restoration in the 1980s.

The **Palazzo dei Conservatori** contains more classical sculpture. In the courtyard are fragments of the colossal statue of Constantine (4th century AD), and in the gallery are the *Spinario* (a 1st century bc bronze of a boy taking a thorn from his foot) and the *Capitoline Wolf* (Etruscan, 5th century BC). The figures of the suckling twins, Romulus and Remus, were added in 1498 by Antonio Pollaiuolo, a talented Florentine artist and goldsmith. The home of this statue, the early symbol of Rome, has always been the Capitoline; it was here in 65BC that lightning damaged the wolf's hindquarters.

On the second floor is the Pinacoteca Capitolina, with paintings by Veronese, Guercino, Tintoretto, Rubens, Caravaggio, Van Dyck, Titian and Pietro da Cortona; . *Both palaces are in the Piazza del Campidoglio (tel: 671 02071). Open: Tuesday to Saturday, 9am–1.30pm and 5–8pm; Sunday, 9am–1pm; April to September, Saturday, 8am–11pm; October to March, Saturday, 5–8pm. Closed Monday. Admission charge (ticket valid for both parts of the museum), free on the last Sunday of the month. Bus: 44, 94, 710, 718, 719.*

MUSEO DELLA CIVILTÀ ROMANA (Museum of Roman Culture)
This museum is housed in the Palazzo della Civiltà del Lavoro at EUR (see page 40). It traces the history of the city using models, including a vast scale-model of Rome as it was in the days of Constantine showing everything contained within the Aurelian Walls (see page 32).

Piazza G Agnelli, EUR (tel: 592 6135). Open: Tuesday to Saturday, 9am–1pm; Sunday, 9am–1pm; also Tuesday and Thursday, 4–7pm. Admission charge. Bus: 93, 97, 197, 293, 493, 765. Metro: EUR Fermi, EUR Palasport.

MUSEO DELLE MURA (Museum of the Walls)
Housed within the medieval towers of the Porta San Sebastiano (see page 71), the Museo delle Mura unravels the history of the Aurelian Walls (see page 32) and the Via Appia Antica (see page 116). There are prints and models and a magnificent view out over the ancient landscape surrounding the Via Appia Antica.
Via di Porta San Sebastiano 18 (tel: 70 47 5284). Open: Tuesday to Saturday, 9am–1.30pm; Sunday, 9am–1pm; also April to September, Tuesday, Thursday and Saturday, 4–7pm. Admission charge. Bus: 118.

The dismembered Constantine is the much-loved resident of Palazzo dei Conservatori's courtyard

What did they wear? And what did they look like? These are some of the questions answered at the Museo della Civiltà Romana

MUSEO NAZIONALE DELLE ARTI E TRADIZIONI POPOLARI (Museum of Folklore and Folk Art)

The Museum of Folklore brings alive a now-vanished way of life, with sections devoted to costumes, folk art, agriculture and old musical instruments.

Piazza Marconi 10, EUR (tel: 5926148). Open: Monday to Saturday, 9am–2pm; Sunday, 9am–1pm . Admission charge. Bus: 93, 97, 197, 293, 493, 765. Metro: EUR Fermi, EUR Palasport.

MUSEO NAZIONALE ETRUSCO (Etruscan Museum)

The Villa Giulia contains the best collection of Etruscan art and artefacts in Italy, much of it from excavations in Lazio and Tuscany. It is a treasure house of jewellery, plate, bronzes, vases, sarcophagi and household objects, grouped according to where they were found. The Etruscans' most prized possessions were placed in their tombs for use in the afterlife, which explains their excellent state of preservation. The precious Castellani Collection, donated by the Castellani family in 1919, is unlocked for private viewing if you leave identification at the ticket desk.

The villa itself is a splendid building, constructed for Pope Julius III as a summer retreat. Michelangelo was probably consulted on the design, but the work is Giacomo Barozzi Vignola's (1551–3). Bartolommeo Ammanati designed the loggia at the end of the courtyard, and in the garden is Vignola's nymphaeum, a water-garden decorated with mosaics, statues and fountains. Although the pope never lived here, he filled it with sculpture, 160 boatloads of which were sent to the Vatican when he died in 1555.

Piazzale di Villa Giulia 9 (tel: 322 6571). Open: Tuesday and Thursday to Saturday, 9am–7pm (October to March, until 2pm); Wednesday, 9am–7pm; Sunday, 9am–1pm. Closed 1 Jan, 1 May, 25 Dec. Admission charge. Bus: 52, 926, 95, 490.

MUSEO NAZIONALE PREISTORICO ED ETNOGRAFICO (Prehistoric and Ethnographic Museum)

This museum covers the Stone, Bronze and Iron Ages, with a special section devoted to Lazio and the Etruscans.

Viale Lincoln 1, EUR (tel: 5923057).
Open: summer, Monday to Saturday,
9am–7pm; winter, Monday to Saturday,
9am–2pm; Sunday, 9am–1pm all year.
Admission charge. Bus: 93, 97, 197, 293,
493, 765. Metro: EUR Fermi, EUR
Palasport.

MUSEO DI PALAZZO VENEZIA
(Museum of the Palace of Venice)

The best way to see inside the ancient
Palazzo Venezia is to visit the museum
housed there. It contains a
comprehensive collection of medieval art,
early Renaissance paintings and bronzes,
tapestries, weapons, majolica, jewellery,
silver and Neapolitan crib figures.
Sculpture includes some in terracotta by
Bernini and a marble screen from the
Aracoeli convent, torn down when the
Monumento Vittorio Emanuele was
built. Temporary exhibitions are also
held here, their presence announced by a
banner hung on the façade.

The Palazzo Venezia was Mussolini's
headquarters and from its first-floor
balcony he would harangue the crowds
below. His office occupied the vast Sala
di Mappamondo (the Hall of the Map of
the World – painted on the ceiling) on
the first floor. At night he would leave
the lights on to give the impression to the
outside world that he worked all night
long. The reality was quite different – his
mistress was installed in the next room.

The palace, completed in 1467 for
Cardinal Pietro Barbo (later Pope Paul
II), was the first great Renaissance palace
to be erected in Rome. Barbo was
Venetian, a connection which led
eventually to the palace becoming the
Embassy of the Venetian Republic until
1797. It is appropriate that the museum,
established in 1985, should be here, for
Paul II was a patron of scholars and an

insatiable collector of objets d'art .
Via del Plebiscito 118 (tel: 679–8865).
Open: summer, Monday to Saturday,
9am–7.30pm; winter, Tuesday to Saturday,
9am–2pm; Sunday, 9am–1pm all year.
Admission charge. Bus: 56, 60, 64, 70, 75.

Mussolini's headquarters – the Palazzo Venezia
flanks the loggia of San Marco

Michelangelo's cloister now houses part of the Museo Nazionale's huge collection of Roman antiquities

MUSEO NAZIONALE ROMANO
(National Museum of Roman
Antiquities)

This is one of Rome's most important museums of antiquities and one of the world's leading repositories of classical art. Like the church of Santa Maria degli Angeli (see page 82), it is located within the magnificent halls of the Baths of Diocletian (see page 91), which provide a remarkable setting for antique sculpture, carvings, mosaics and frescos. The museum is subject to intermittent closures so it is impossible to guarantee entry (check with the ticket office).

On the first floor is the Ludovisi Throne (or is it an altar?), possibly depicting Aphrodite being lifted from the sea by two of her priestesses. In the Great Cloister, reputed to be

Michelangelo's last architectural project, is the magnificent 2nd-century AD *Discobolus* , a copy of a Greek original and one of the best preserved antique statues anywhere. Other sculptures include the *Girl of Anzio* and the *Venus of Cyrene*, her clothes flung over a dolphin with a fish in its mouth. The *Niobid* , an original Greek work (460–430BC), may have come from the pediment of a Greek temple, while best of all is the *Boxer,* a magnificent bronze dating from around the 2nd century BC.

On the second floor are stuccos and wall paintings taken from the remains of an ancient villa (thought to be where Caesar kept his mistress Cleopatra) discovered in the grounds of the Villa Farnesina and from the Domus Flavia on the Palatino. An exquisite room decorated with *trompe-l'œil* birds and flowers came from the villa at Prima Porta belonging to Augustus and Livia. *Viale Enrico de Nicola 79 (tel: 48 90 3507). Open: Tuesday to Saturday, 9am–2pm; Sunday and public holidays, 9am–1pm. Admission charge. Bus: 57, 65, 75, 170. Metro: Repubblica.*

MUSEO DI ROMA (Museum of Rome)

The Museo di Roma is in the Palazzo Braschi, built at the end of the 18th century for the unpleasant nephew of Pope Pius VI, Duke Onesti-Braschi. He once quelled an anti-papal riot by flinging gold coins out of his windows into the mob, then beating the scrambling figures with dog whips. In 1952 the palace became a museum dedicated to the history of Rome since the Middle Ages. Its outstanding exhibits are the fragments of frescos and mosaics from the old basilica of St Peter's. There are busts and portraits of popes and cardinals, and views of the city through the ages.
Piazza San Pantaleo 10 (tel: 686 5696). Open: Tuesday to Sunday 10am–1pm (Tuesday and Thursday also 5-7.30pm). Bus: 46, 62, 64, 70, 81, 87, 90.

ORATORIO DEI FILIPPINI (Oratory of the Filippini)

That most charitable of mystics St Philip Neri founded the religious order of the Filippini in 1575, during the Counter-Reformation. Their Oratory lies next to the Chiesa Nuova (see page 86) in a building designed by Borromini (1637–43), unusual for the concave curve of its façade.

The Filippini were a brotherhood of laymen who went about Rome comforting the sick in hospitals, looking after pilgrims and making pilgrimages to the seven major basilicas, all in an effort to inject a little spirituality into a city demoralised after its 1527 sack. The 'oratorio' – the performance of religious music sung, often in dramatic form, by solo voices and chorus – was developed here.

Today the building houses the **Archivio Capitolino** and the **Biblioteca Vallicelliana**, and these can be visited along with the Oratory itself (ask the porter for the key). The Oratory is sometimes used for concerts.
Piazza della Chiesa Nuova (tel: 686 9374). Open most mornings but phone to check. Bus: 46, 62, 64, 70. 81, 87, 90.

Borromini's curvaceous façade of the Oratorio dei Filippini

Giants of the Baroque

The baroque style first appeared in Rome at the start of the 17th century, reaching its apogee during the pontificate of Urban VIII. The three great Roman artists of the baroque, Bernini (poet, playwright, composer, sculptor and painter), Borromini (Bernini's great rival, a creative, eccentric genius with a passion for archaeology) and Cortona (master of architecture and painting and a learned theologian), gave brilliant expression to a style imitated all over Europe.

GIAN LORENZO BERNINI (1598–1680)

Bernini virtually created the baroque with his imaginative use of coloured marbles, bronze and stucco, his combination of sensuality and mysticism and the sense of movement and immediacy he gave to his subjects. For more than 20 years he was artistic dictator of Rome, jealously guarded by his Barberini patrons. His authority dominated all the arts, and was responsible for the relative neglect of Borromini.

FRANCESCO BORROMINI (1599–1667)

Bernini said that the quarrelsome, neurotic Borromini 'had been sent to destroy architecture'. For centuries much vilified as a wild revolutionary, he is now recognised as one of the masters of the baroque for his originality.

PIETRO DA CORTONA (1596–1669)

Like Bernini, Cortona created some of his greatest works for the Barberini. Two major influences on his painting were Raphael and Titian; from the first he acquired an aptitude for 'free' design, from the second a warmth of colour. Together, these were the foundation stone on which baroque painting was established.

MICHELANGELO MERISI DA CARAVAGGIO (1573–1610)

Caravaggio was one of the most significant painters to emerge between Michelangelo and Rembrandt. His eventful sojourn in Rome came to an end in 1606 when, having killed someone in a brawl, he fled only to die after another fight. The darker side of his character is reflected in his unorthodox paintings, notable for their vivid realism.

Bernini's *St Peter Enthroned*, in the Basilica di San Pietro

Palatino

(The Palatine)

For the background, see page 28.

CAPANNA DI ROMOLO (Romulus' Hut)

In the 1940s evidence of Iron Age habitation was unearthed on the Palatine, suggesting that here was none other than the site of the settlement founded by Romulus in 753BC.

CASA DI LIVIA (Livia's House)

Livia, third wife of Emperor Augustus, may have lived here, though in all probability the building was simply a 1st-century BC extension of Augustus' palace. However, lead pipes bearing Livia's name were discovered here. Its rooms were most sumptuous if the surviving decorations are anything to go by. It contained the customary *atrium,* or forecourt, leading to a *triclinium* (dining room) with a nearby tablinum (open saloon). Wonderful wall paintings of mythological scenes, landscapes and cityscapes, and other decorative interior effects have survived and can be seen *in situ.*

DOMUS AUGUSTANA AND STADIO DOMIZIANO (Domitian's Stadium)

'Augustana' relates to the 'august' emperors whose palace stood on the Palatine and remained in use until the passing of the Byzantine era. This was the emperor's private residence as opposed to the Domus Flavia, its other wing, which was his official one and seat of the imperial government. Both were part of a vast complex of palaces and gardens built by Emperor Domitian on a prominent site overlooking the Forum on one side and the Circus Maximus on the other. It was a magnificent establishment adorned with the richest marbles and filled with fountains (note the oval fountain which was designed to be seen from the palace's dining hall), statues, sunken gardens, temples and decorated apartments. Not much remains today apart from some fragments of wall, column and marble floor. Of the Stadio Domiziano, attached to the Domus Augustana, not much is known and it may simply have been a sunken garden. Theodoric, the Ostrogoth king, held footraces here in the 6th century (the oval enclosure at the southern end is

On the Palatine: the ruins of the Domus Augustana

his), and it has been suggested that it was earlier used by the emperors for their own private entertainment.

DOMUS SEVERIANA

Of all the ruins on the Palatine, those of the Domus Severiana are the most impressive. Emperor Septimius Severus was one of the most outstanding imperial builders; his Palatine palace, actually an extension of the Domus Augustana, contained a fanciful arrangement of fountains arranged over three tiers of porticoes, and projected beyond the hillside, requiring enormous arched supports which can still be seen today.

DOMUS TIBERIANA

Emperor Tiberius also constructed a residence on the Palatine, though not much has survived. Tiberius' successor Caligula extended the palace west towards the Forum. To the east is the *cryptoporticus*, a half-buried, barrel-vaulted corridor, later built by Nero to link the various Palatine palaces. Legend has it that Caligula and his fourth wife, Caesonia, were stabbed to death here.

ORTI FARNESIANI (Farnese Gardens)

Much of the ruins of the Domus Tiberiana lie buried beneath the Farnese Gardens laid out for Cardinal Alessandro Farnese, grandson of Pope Paul III, by Vignola in the 16th century. In fact Farnese, who bought the ruins of Tiberius' palace, had them filled in so that the garden could be created. It became one of the first botanical gardens in Europe. Excavations in more recent times mean that the garden, though still a pretty place to walk or sit, has lost its former glory.
The Palatino is reached from the Roman Forum (see page 44), or from the Via di

High on the Palatine, the Farnese Gardens are an oasis of tranquillity

San Gregorio (tel: 699 0110). Open: Monday to Saturday, 9am–5pm; Sunday, 9am–noon. Admission charge. Bus: 11, 27, 81, 85, 87. Metro: Colosseo.

The remains of a fountain within the ruins of Domitian's palace

Palazzi

(Palaces)

PALAZZO BORGHESE

This palace, acquired by the Borghese pope Paul V in 1605, was completed by Flaminio Ponzio. Carlo Rainaldi designed the entrance portal and the beautiful courtyard gardens in the 1670s. Napoleon's sister Pauline lived here following her marriage to Prince Camillo Borghese in 1803, and today it is home to Rome's exclusive *Caccia* (Hunt Club). Until 1902 the Borghese art collection was housed here (now at the Galleria Borghese, see page 50).
Largo della Fontanella di Borghese. Not open to the public. Bus: 70, 81, 90, 906.

OTHER PALACES OPEN TO THE PUBLIC
Palazzo Barberini, **Palazzo Corsini** and **Palazzo Doria Pamphili**, see pages 52–3
Palazzo Colonna, see page 51
Palazzo Nuovo and **Palazzo dei Conservatori** see page 57
Palazzo Spada see page 114
Palazzo Venezia see page 59

PALAZZO FARNESE

The finest and stateliest palace in Rome, this is one of the gems of the Renaissance period. Although difficult to visit (it is the French Embassy), its façade and setting are worth seeing. The second act of *Tosca* is set here.

The palace was begun for Cardinal Alessandro Farnese (later Pope Paul III, 1534–49) by Antonio da Sangallo the Younger in 1514. After da Sangallo's death in 1546, Michelangelo took over, adding the upper storey and cornice. He planned a riverside wing and bridge, but only a single arch of the bridge was built over the Via Giulia, linking the palace with the Villa Farnesina (see page 103) in Trastevere.

Inside, the first floor has ceiling frescos, illustrating scenes from Ovid's *Metamorphoses*, by the Carracci brothers, Agostino and Annibale (1597–1603). You can catch a glimpse of the frescos by looking up into the windows from the piazza at night.
Piazza Farnese. Open to the public intermittently – write to The Ambassador, French Embassy, Piazza Farnese 64, 00186, Rome. Bus: 46, 62, 64, 70, 71, 87, 90.

PALAZZO MADAMA

Built in the 16th century, this was originally Medici property: the two Medici popes Giovanni (Leo X), and Giuliano (Clement VII) both lived here as young men. It later became the home of Margherita of Austria, illegitimate daughter of Emperor Charles V and known as Madama. In the 17th century it was enlarged by Maruscelli for Ferdinand II, Grand Duke of Tuscany; the carved window decoration includes the lily of Florence. Since 1871 the palace has been the seat of the Senate (the upper house of the Italian parliament).
Piazza Madama. Not open to the public. Bus: 70, 81, 87, 90, 90b.

PALAZZO DI MONTECITORIO

Begun in 1650 by Bernini for Innocent X, the palace was completed by Carlo

The Palazzo di Montecitorio, crowning the summit of a low hill

Fontana in 1694 for Innocent XII as the seat of the papal courts. In 1871, extended and remodelled, it became the *Camera dei Deputati*, Chamber of Deputies. The curved façade, a novelty introduced by Bernini, survives.
Piazza di Montecitorio. Not open to the public. Bus: 56, 60, 85, 90, 90b.

PALAZZO DEL QUIRINALE

Former summer retreat of the popes and from 1870 to 1944 seat of the kings of Italy, the Quirinale Palace is now the presidential residence.

Pope Gregory XIII (1572–85) first chose this site as an escape from the fetid summer conditions of the Vatican, and many illustrious architects have had a hand in its design, Bernini among them. He was responsible for the Benediction Loggia (1638) over the main entrance in Piazza del Quirinale and the *manica lunga*

('long sleeve'), a long narrow wing running along the Via del Quirinale in which the pope housed his family.
Piazza del Quirinale. For permission to visit the interior, apply to the Ufficio Intendenza, Palazzo del Quirinale, 00137, Rome. Bus: 52, 53, 56, 60, 61, 62.

Seat of the President: the Palazzo Quirinale

From the hand of Michelangelo, the Piazza del Campidoglio

PANTHEON, see the walk on pages 104–5.

PIAZZA DEL CAMPIDOGLIO

This square is the focus of the Capitolino (Capitoline hill, see page 29), the cradle of ancient Rome and still the symbolic heart of the city. The site was in a state of dereliction, when Pope Paul III commissioned Michelangelo to rebuild the piazza: Rome needed a suitably impressive public space in which to receive the Holy Roman Emperor Charles V, who was due to arrive (1536) in triumphal procession following his victory over the infidel in North Africa. It was the obvious place for such a square, and Michelangelo was instructed to design a suitable approach to it. He conceived the gently rising ramp known

as the *Cordonata,* from the cords originally stretched across such ways to give a foothold to animals.

As the centrepiece and focus of the piazza, Michelangelo envisaged the much revered ancient statue of Marcus Aurelius (see page 56), its one hand outstretched to welcome the spectator. He proposed an oval pattern inscribed into the pavement around the statue's plinth, and behind it, facing the *Cordonata,* a restored Palazzo Senatorio (now Rome's town hall). On either side of this would be the slightly canted Palazzo dei Conservatori, also restored and with a stylish new façade, and the Palazzo Nuovo, a brand new building, to balance and mirror it. Michelangelo had conceived a gigantic stage-set for Marcus Aurelius, but it was left to a later

generation to carry out his plans, as he died having completed only the statue's plinth. Palazzo Nuovo was completed in the 17th century. The large statues of Castor and Pollux at the head of the Cordonata were found in the *Teatro di Pompei* (Theatre of Pompey) during the pontificate of Pius IV and placed here in 1583. Goethe said of the square on his last day in Rome in 1788, that it was like 'an enchanted palace in a desert'.
Bus: 44, 46, 56, 60, 64, 65, 70, 75.

PIAZZA SAN PIETRO

Of all Rome's squares, this is the most theatrical and dramatic. It is the work of Bernini for the Chigi pope Alexander VII, a devout and intellectual man who on the very day of his election in 1655 asked Bernini to enter his service.

Bernini found an awkward site, dominated by an enormous Egyptian obelisk brought to Rome from Heliopolis by Caligula in AD37 and erected in the now lost *Circus Neronis* on the Vatican hill. Pope Sixtus V had it resited (with difficulty since it weighed over 500 tonnes) in 1586. A golden ball, long thought to contain the ashes of Julius Caesar, was removed and replaced with a bronze cross containing a relic of the Holy Cross.

Bernini had to reckon with this old established landmark. He also had to consider that as many people as possible in the square should be able to see the Benediction Loggia above the central entrance to the Basilica of St Peter's (see page 88) and the Pope's window in the Vatican Palace to the right. Bernini's ingenious solution was a double colonnade which encircles the piazza and symbolically embraces the faithful. Originally the piazza was entered from a narrow street, and the viewer was

suddenly thrust into the vast encircled amphitheatre. This effect was ruined by Mussolini when he drove the much vilified Via della Conciliazione (commemorating the ending of the 80-year-old division between Church and State) through the Borgo (see page 33). *Bus: 64.*

PIAZZA DEL POPOLO, see page 118.

The dome of St Peter's dominates the Piazza San Pietro, soaring way above the rooftops of Rome

PORTE DI ROMA (Rome's Gates)

Many of Rome's old gateways through the Aurelian Wall (see page 32) survive. Some of the most interesting are described below.

Porta Asinaria

The 'Gate of the Donkeys', a minor gate with twin circular towers, is as old as the Wall itself. The Ostrogothic king Totila entered Rome this way in AD546, let in by treacherous barbarian soldiers in the Roman army. It was reopened recently having been closed since 1409.
Between Piazza di S Giovanni and Piazzale Appio. Bus: 4, 15, 16, 81, 85, 87, Metro: San Giovanni.

Porta Maggiore

A more splendid ancient gateway is Porta Maggiore, constructed by Emperor Claudius in AD52 and incorporated into the Aurelian Wall in 279. It marked the junction of roads leading to Palestrina and Cassino, the remains of which can still be seen. The two arches carried the Acqua Claudia and Anio Novus, two aqueducts bringing water from Subiaco 68km away.
Piazza di Porta Maggiore. Bus: 105.

Porta Pia

Michelangelo's last architectural design (his is the main block), the gate was built into the Aurelian Wall between 1561 and 1564 and reconstructed 1853–61. Until a century ago there was countryside beyond. The Wall was breached here by the armies of a united Italy on 20 September 1870. The building contains the small **Museo dei Bersaglieri**, which contains military memorabilia.
Via XX Settembre. Bus: 36, 36b, 37, 60, 62.

Keats' grave in the Protestant Cemetery

Porta San Paolo

This was once called the Porta Ostiense because the road from it led to Ostia (see page 1270, passing *en route* the Basilica di San Paolo Fuori le Mura (see page 87), from which the gate now takes its name. Built by Aurelian in the 3rd century, it has a façade added by Emperor Honorius in AD402, and a tower built by Belisarius in the 6th century. In the gatehouse is the **Museo della Via Ostiense** containing a small collection of finds excavated along this old route.

Piazza di Porta San Paolo.

Porta San Sebastiano

The Porta Appia of antiquity, this is the finest of the Aurelian gateways. It was built in the 3rd century at the head of the Via Appia (see pages 116–17), replacing the even older Porta Capena, part of the Servian Wall. Honorius restored it in the 5th century as did Narsus and Belisarius again in the 6th. The two battlemented towers are medieval. The gate contains the **Museo delle Mura** (see page 57).

Via Appia Antica. Bus: 118.

PORTICO D'OTTAVIA

This was a vast rectangular portico enclosing temples dedicated to Jupiter

The Porta Pia, gateway to Rome

and Juno. Among the 270 columns stood masterpieces of Greek sculpture, including the Medici Venus now in the Uffizi Gallery in Florence. It was rebuilt by Augustus and dedicated to his sister Octavia in 23BC. Surviving columns surround the entrance to the church of Sant'Angelo in Pescheria (founded 770), built into the ruins. The medieval fish market, the *Forum Piscarium*, was held in the portico.

Via del Portico d'Ottavia. Bus: 57, 90, 90b, 92, 94, 95

PROTESTANTE, CIMITERO (Protestant Cemetery)

John Keats, the ashes of Percy Bysshe Shelley and Goethe's illegitimate son Julius Augustus are all buried here, as are some 4,000 non-Catholic Italians, including the founder of the Italian Communist Party, Antonio Gramsci. A map of who lies where can be obtained from the caretaker. Near by is the ancient Piramide di Caio Cestio (12BC), a vast stone pyramid which is the grandiose tomb of an otherwise unexceptional Roman.

Cimitero Protestante, Via Caio Cestio 6 (tel: 574 1141). Open: summer, 8am–noon and 3.30–5.30pm; winter, 8am–noon and 2.30–4.30pm; closed Wednesday all year. Bus: 11, 23, 27, 57, 94, 95. Metro: Piramide.

ROME'S CHURCHES

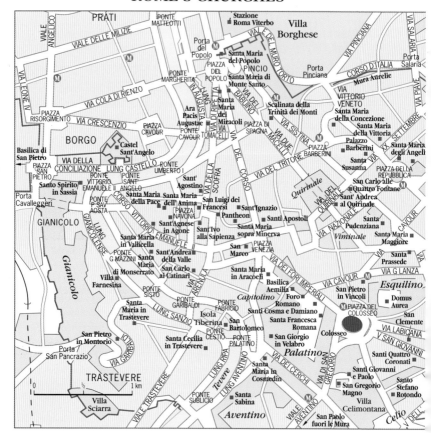

SANT'AGNESE FUORI LE MURA
(St Agnes outside the Walls)

St Agnes was only 13 when she was martyred as a Christian in 304. She is said to have refused marriage to a pagan, preferring to consecrate her virginity to God. For this decision she was sent to a brothel, where her hair miraculously grew until it covered her. One soldier tried to rape her – it is said –

and he was struck blind. Eventually Agnese was done away with, beheaded by Diocletian. She was was buried here, outside the walls. The church marks her tomb and was built by Princess Constantia the Great's granddaughter, some time before 349.

The Basilica of Sant'Agnese fuori le Mura, restored by Honorius 1, who had been pope from 625–638, preserves an

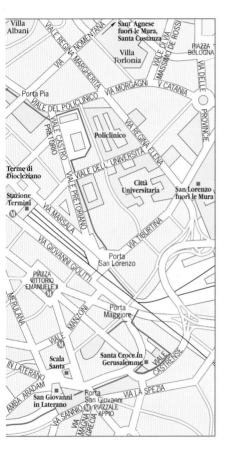

A different order of visitor

air of early Christian mystery in spite of 19th-century restorations. The 16 columns (removed from a much earlier classical building), *matroneum* (women's gallery) above them and four ancient porphyry columns supporting the altar canopy date from the 7th century. Sant'Agnese herself is depicted in the 7th-century apse mosaic. Beneath the church is a 4th-century catacomb within 7km of tunnels which can be seen on request to the sacristan.

Via Nomentana 349 (tel: 861 0840). Open: Monday and Wednesday to Saturday, 9am–noon and 4–6pm; Sunday, 4–6pm. Catacombs also closed on Monday. Admission charge to catacombs. Bus: 36, 36b, 37, 60.

SANT'AGNESE IN AGONE, see page 111.

SANT'AGOSTINO
This is one of Rome's earliest Renaissance churches (1479–83, redecorated in the 18th century). Its chief glory is Caravaggio's *Madonna di Loreto* of 1605 (bottom chapel, left-hand aisle), with the dirty feet of a worshipping pilgrim much to the fore. This, together with the peasant-like Virgin and the naked Christ, scandalised those who saw the work at its unveiling.

Just inside the church entrance is

The result of much rebuilding over the centuries, Santi Apostoli dominates Piazza Santi Apostoli

Jacopo Sansovino's *Madonna del Parto* (*Madonna of the Childbirth*, completed in 1521), much revered by expectant mothers and couples wanting a child, as the votive offerings lining its niche and the much-kissed foot of the Madonna testify. Sansovino's *Madonna and Child with St Anne* is against the third column on the left, beneath Raphael's *Prophet Isaiah* (both from 1512).
Piazza di Sant'Agostino. Bus: 70, 81, 87, 90, 90b.

SANT'ANDREA AL QUIRINALE, see page 109.

SANT'ANDREA DELLA VALLE
This church, best known as scene of the first act of Puccini's *Tosca*, contains a startling baroque painting. Giovanni Lanfranco's dome fresco, *The Glory of Paradise* (1625–8), was an exuberant novelty which shocked and titillated in equal measure. Lanfranco's rival, Domenichino, painted the four Evangelists in the dome's pendentives and scenes from the life of St Andrew in the choir (1624–8). So jealous was Domenichino of Lanfranco's having the better commission that, so the story goes, he weakened the scaffolding on which the latter was working, hoping Lanfranco would plunge to his death.

The church, begun in 1591, partially completed by Carlo Maderno (architect of the façade of St Peter's) in 1621, was finally given a façade in the 1660s. Of early baroque design – rich, ornamented and statuesque – this is part Maderno's, part Carlo Rainaldi's and part Domenico Fontana's. It glows from a recent face-lift.
Corso Vittorio Emanuele/Piazza S Andrea della Valle. Bus: 46, 62, 64, 70, 81, 87, 90, 90b.

SANTI APOSTOLI

The church here is nearly 1,500 years old and was probably founded by Pope Pelagius; however, it was virtually completely rebuilt in the 18th century. The only indications of its great age are the fluted columns in the Cappella del Crocifisso (at the end of the south aisle).

The handsome portico contains a tomb by Canova (1807) and inside, at the end of the left aisle, the same sculptor's monument to Pope Clement XIV (1789). In the right aisle (second pier left) is a monument to Clementina Sobieska, mother of Bonnie Prince Charlie, and in the basement are tombs of the Apostles James and Philip (hence the church's name).

Piazza dei Santi Apostoli. Bus: 56, 60, 64, 65, 70, 75, 85, 90.

Above: Sant'Andrea della Valle has just been restored and is gleaming white
Below: Sant'Agostino contains work by Sansovino, Raphael and Caravaggio

SAN BARTOLOMEO ALL'ISOLA
(St Bartholomew on the Island)

This church located on the Tiber Island (see page 54) occupies the site of the ancient Temple of Aesculapius, god of healing. The present building, built by Emperor Otto III, dates back at least to the late 10th century when it was dedicated to St Adalbert. Inside, on the chancel steps, is a Romanesque wellhead which may mark the site of the earlier temple's healing spring. In the Middle Ages a pilgrim's hospice grew up on the island; indeed a hospital survives there now. Continually damaged by the flooding river, San Bartolomeo was rebuilt in the 16th century. The principal relic here is the remains of San Bartolomeo, brought to Rome by Otto III in the copper dish seen behind the grill on the right of the chancel. The saint is buried in the ancient porphyry vessel which doubles as high altar.

Piazza S Bartolomeo all'Isola. Buses to Isola Tiberina: 15, 23, 97, 780.

Santa Cecilia was built on the site of the home of the early Christian saint of the same name

tomb was opened, she was found miraculously preserved, wrapped in a golden robe; her executioner's botched attempts at beheading her (he tried and failed three times, so that in the end she died of her wounds) were evidenced by gashes in her neck. Stefano Maderno drew her as found and the statue beneath the high altar is the result.

Traces of the early building and its decoration survive: the gallery above the entrance houses the remains of Pietro Cavallini's fresco *The Last Judgement* (1293), a masterpiece of medieval art. The apse mosaic (9th-century) depicts Paschal I being introduced to Christ in Heaven by St Cecilia.

Piazza di S Cecilia. Admission charge for excavations. Cavallini fresco can be seen Tuesday and Thursday, 10–11.30am. Bus: 56, 60, 75, 710.

SAN CLEMENTE

A microcosm of the history of Rome, San Clemente was built before 385. The earliest level of the site contains ancient Roman remains, including a Mithraic shrine and a 1st-century house, part of which was used for secret early Christian worship. Both can be seen beneath the church.

The lower church was restored in the 8th and 9th centuries but destroyed in 1084 by the Normans and excavated 800 years later. Faded 9th-century frescos can still be seen, including an inscription thought to be the earliest example of written Italian. In 1108 Paschal II built the upper church, which was reconstructed in the 18th century. Behind the altar a magnificent 12th-century mosaic depicts *The Triumph of*

SAN CARLO AI CATINARI

This vast baroque church, rejoicing under the name St Charles of the Washtub Makers, was completed between 1611 and 1646 for Cardinal Scipione Borghese (see page 50) in honour of the newly canonised Milanese, St Charles Borromeo. It contains paintings by Domenichino, Cortona, Reni, Lanfranco and Sacchi.

Piazza B Cairoli. Bus: 44, 56, 60, 65, 75.

SAN CARLO ALLE QUATTRO
FONTANE, see page 109.

SANTA CECILIA IN TRASTEVERE

This interesting church built by Pope Paschal I (817–24), was 'modernised' in the 18th, 19th and 20th centuries. The campanile and the portico (with its antique columns) were added in the 12th century.

The hideously martyred St Cecilia lived here. In the 16th century, when her

Santa Cecilia, horribly martyred, is the patron saint of music

the Cross. The interior is dominated by the *schola cantorum* (a 6th-century choir enclosure) and a beautiful inlaid marble pavement. In the Cappella di Santa Caterina is Masolino's *Life of Santa Caterina* (c.1428), a rare example of the work of this early Renaissance artist. Since 1667, San Clemente has been the seat of the Irish Dominicans.
Via di San Giovanni in Laterano. Bus: 81, 85, 87, 93. Metro: Colosseo.

SANTA COSTANZA

This little circular church was built in the 4th century as a mausoleum, probably for Emperor Constantine's daughters Helena and Constantina. The most complete building of Constantine's time, Santa Costanza has beautiful lively contemporary mosaics in the ambulatory.
Via Nomentana. Bus: 36, 36b, 37, 60.

SANTA CROCE IN GERUSALEMME (The Holy Cross in Jerusalem)

Traditionally said to have been founded by the Emperor Constantine, the church is known to have existed in the 4th

century. It has been rebuilt and restored many times: the present campanile is 12th century and the façade 17th century. The church is of great interest for its relics, brought to Rome from Palestine by Constantine's mother Empress Helena. There are pieces of the True Cross, two holy thorns, a nail, the INRI label from the cross and a great beam alleged to be part of the good thief's cross. Even the floor of the chapel in the vaults is packed with Jerusalem soil.
Piazza di Santa Croce in Gerusalemme. Bus: 9.

San Clemente, with its mosaics, is one of the oldest churches in Rome

One of Rome's most impressive churches, San Giovanni in Laterano was transformed by Borromini

SAN GIOVANNI IN LATERANO

Rome's main cathedral church, this is the Pope's titular seat as Bishop of Rome. Alessandro Galilei's dramatic entrance façade of 1735 is crowned by gigantic statues of Christ, John the Baptist, John the Evangelist and the 12 Doctors of the Church. The central bronze doors come from the ancient senate house in the Foro Romano.

Emperor Constantine built the first church here (314–18) over army barracks in a palace that then stood on the site. The Vandals, earthquakes and fire destroyed this and later churches, then in 1586 the core of what can be seen now was begun. Borromini was responsible for the interior (1646). The church retains its original basilical shape; within, there is a Gothic tabernacle (1367) over the high altar (at which only the Pope can say Mass) accompanied by a wooden table said to be that used by St Peter and the earliest popes. The relics venerated here are the skulls of St Peter and St Paul.

San Giovanni's 13th-century cloisters are remarkable for their twisted columns and their Cosmati decoration, but the most interesting feature of the whole complex is the Baptistery, dating from 432 and the only part of the earliest church to have survived. Its design and plan – a vaulted octagon – provided the model for all subsequent baptisteries throughout Italy. *Piazza di San Giovanni in Laterano (tel: 698 643). Church and cloister open: daily, 7am–7pm (October to March, until 6pm). Baptistery open: daily, 9am–1pm and 4–6pm. Museum open: Monday to Friday, 9am–1pm and 3–5pm. Admission charge for cloister and museum. Bus: 4, 15, 16, 85, 87, 93. Metro: San Giovanni.*

SANTI GIOVANNI E PAOLO and
SAN GREGORIO MAGNO, see page
113.

SANT'IGNAZIO

The ceiling decorations here, by Andrea
Pozzo (1642–1709), are dazzling. They
illustrate the missionary activity of the
Jesuits (founded by St Ignatius Loyola),
for whom Orazio Grassi designed this
vast church. The dome was never built,
but the painted false perspective gives
the impression that it was. Finest of all
is the nave fresco *The Glory of
Sant'Ignazio* (finished 1694), best seen
from the marble disc in the middle of
the nave.
*Via di Sant'Ignazio. Bus: 56, 60, 71, 81,
85, 90.*

SANT'IVO ALLA SAPIENZA, see
page 108.

SAN LORENZO FUORI LE MURA

The first basilica was built by
Constantine over the tomb of St
Lawrence who, in 258, was roasted to
death on a gridiron. Pope Pelagius II
rebuilt it in the 6th century, and 200
years later it was linked to a nearby
church dedicated to the Virgin. Honorius
III enlarged the church in 1216, and the
nave, the portico (damaged in World
War II and subsequently rebuilt) and
most of the decoration date from his
period.

The choir mosaic depicts Pelagius
donating the church to Christ. The crypt
contains the relics of SS Lorenzo,
Stefano and Justino.
*Piazzale del Verano. Bus: 36, 36b, 37, 60,
136.*

SAN LUIGI DEI FRANCESI, see
page 108.

SAN MARCO (St Mark's)

This is one of Rome's oldest basilicas.
The 4th-century Pope Mark founded it,
and the Venetian Pope Paul II
reconstructed it in the 15th century,
when he built the adjacent Palazzo
Venezia (see page 59). Its best features
are a 9th-century mosaic in the apse,
showing Pope Gregory IV presenting
the basilica to Christ with St Mark and
other saints; Paul II's gilded ceiling; and
the portico where the celebrants of
outdoor Masses could shelter in bad
weather.
*Piazza Venezia. Bus: any to Piazza
Venezia: 56, 60, 64, 65, 70, 75.*

Everything inside San Giovanni in Laterano is
on a huge scale

CHURCH ARCHITECTURE

The great early Christian basilicas – San Paolo fuori le Mura, Santa Maria Maggiore, San Giovanni in Laterano, and Santa Sabina – are ghosts of the ancient Roman public meeting halls: simple and stately with a colonnade separating nave from aisles. Their contemporaries, Santa Costanza (originally a mausoleum) and the Lateran Baptistery, are circular and more intimate in scale. The basilica tradition survived into the 12th century in Santa Maria in Cosmedin and San Clemente. Santa Maria sopra Minerva is a rare example in Rome of the Gothic tradition.

The Renaissance is exemplified in Bramante's designs for the basilica of San Pietro. His classical circular Tempietto in the courtyard of San Pietro in Montorio epitomises the High Renaissance with its perfect proportions and symmetry.

With the Counter-Reformation and the reassertion of church power in the

Left: the approach to San Paolo fuori le Mura
Below: the cloister, San Paolo fuori le Mura

second half of the 16th century, long
naves provided a setting for processions.
The Gesù, with its wide nave and barrel-
vaulted ceiling, was ideal for the preaching
purposes of the newly founded Jesuits.
Its façade was subsequently imitated all
over Europe. Great cycles of decoration
preached the mysteries of the Faith (eg
in the Cappella Sistina in Santa Maria
Maggiore) or the virtues of the martyrs
(the martyrdom frescos in Santo
Stefano Rotondo).

After the Counter-Reformation, the
17th-century baroque was a period of
fulfilment and enjoyment. Architects
preferred curves to straight lines, and
complex forms to regular and simple
ones. The oval was favoured, as in
Bernini's Sant'Andrea al Quirinale.
Façades were made as sculptural as
possible, stressing contrasts of light
and shadow. The interior decoration of
Borromini's San Carlo alle Quattro

Top: curves and counter-curves at Santa
Maria della Pace
Bottom: the cloister, San Paolo fuori le Mura

Fontane and Sant'Ivo alla Sapienza and
Pietro da Cortona's Santi Luca e Martina
and Santa Maria della Pace all show
how piety was sought by providing
drama and a direct appeal to the
emotions.

122 steps lead up to Santa Maria in Aracoeli in which Pinturicchio's frescos are its greatest treasures

SANTA MARIA DEGLI ANGELI

This huge barn-like church (1563), fashioned out of the *frigidarium* of the Báths of Diocletian (see page 91), retains almost nothing by its original designer, Michelangelo. Vanvitelli set to work on it in the 18th century, but was much less careful than his predecessor to preserve the character of the Roman building: the sacristy has an exhibition of Michelangelo's original intentions. There is little of artistic interest apart from a huge statue of St Bruno by Jean-Antoine Houdon and a fresco of the *Martyrdom of St Sebastian* by Domenichino.
Via Cernaia. Bus: 57, 65, 75, 170. Metro: Repubblica.

SANTA MARIA DELL'ANIMA

Built as the German national church in 1431–3, Santa Maria dell'Anima was rebuilt in the 16th century. It contains important 17th-century tombs and frescos, as well as Giulio Romano's (c.1499–1546) *The Holy Family* over the

High Altar. In the choir is Baldassare Peruzzi's tomb of the Dutch Pope Adrian IV (1524–29), once tutor to Emperor Charles V and the last non-Italian Pope before John Paul II.
Via dell'Anima. Bus: 70, 81, 87, 90, 90b, 186, 492.

SANTA MARIA IN ARACOELI

This church on the Capitolino occupies perhaps the most highly venerated site in Rome (see page 29), where Emperor Augustus' Ara Coeli (Altar of Heaven) and other sacred shrines, including the Temple of Juno Moneta, patroness of state finances, once stood. The present structure dates from 1260, when the Franciscans took over the church, and the 122 steps leading up to it were a thanksgiving for deliverance from the Black Death (1348).

The interior splendours were gathered together over the centuries: 22 antique columns from various classical buildings (look for the inscription on the third on the left, which reads '*a cubiculo Augustorum*' – 'from the bedroom of the Emperors'); a gilded wooden ceiling celebrating Colonna's victory at Lepanto (1571); and the fine inlaid marble pavement and pulpits. But the church is visited chiefly for the magnificent Cappella Bufalini (first in the right-hand aisle) with frescos of the *Life of San Bernardino* by Pinturicchio and Benozzo Gozzoli's *St Anthony of Padua* (third chapel on the left). In the south transept is Arnolfo di Cambio's tomb of Luca Savelli (13th century).

The chief object of veneration used to be the Santo Bambino. This figure of a baby, carved from the wood of a Gethsemane olive tree, is supposed to have miraculous healing powers and would be rushed across Rome in a coach (in later times in a taxi) to perform its miracles. Sadly, it was stolen in 1994.
Piazza d'Aracoeli. Bus: 44, 46, 56, 60, 64, 65, 70, 75.

SANTA MARIA DELLA CONCEZIONE

Built for the Capuchin friar Cardinal Antonio Barberini, brother of Pope Urban VIII, the church contains Guido Reni's *St Michael Trampling the Devil. The Devil* bears an uncanny resemblance to the Barberinis' arch rival, the Pamphili Pope Innocent X, and the painting caused an uproar when it was unveiled. But the chief attraction of this church (built around 1624) is a chamber of horrors housed in its crypt, where bones of 4,000 Capuchin monks are decoratively arranged around the walls.
Via Veneto 7. Bus: 52, 53, 56, 58, 58b. Metro: Barberini.

SANTA MARIA IN COSMEDIN

Originally constructed in the 6th century on the site of a classical temple dedicated to Ceres, the church was completed in 1124. Its artistic treasures include a lovely 13th-century altar canopy and a raised choir, but its fame rests on the Bocca della Verità ('mouth of truth') in the porch (see page 121).

At Santa Maria in Cosmedin, the Bocca della Verità is said to bite the hands off liars

SANTA MARIA MAGGIORE

Santa Maria Maggiore stands on the Esquiline Hill where a cult of Juno Lucina, the mother goddess, had been based: the site was thought appropriate for a basilica dedicated to the Virgin Mary, mother of Christ. Rome's finest example of an early Christian basilica, it contains wonderful 5th-century mosaics. The most sacred relics are pieces of wood and metal bands supposedly from the Christchild's crib; an enormous statue of Pope Paul IX kneels before the reliquary, near the altar.

The façade fronting Via Cavour is the work of Ferdinand Fuga (1740). The main entrance, facing Piazza di Santa Maria Maggiore, built for Pope Clement X (1670–6), has a deep arched *loggia* where heretical books were burned in the

SNOW IN SUMMER

The first church on the Esquiline Hill has long vanished. Pope Liberius (352-66) built it after the Virgin appeared to him in a dream one August night, commanding that a church should be built where snow would fall on the next day. A ceremony held every 5 August in the Capella Paolina in Santa Maria Maggiore, when petals are scattered from the dome, commemorates the event.

Virgin's honour. In front is a column from the Basilica of Maxentius (in the Foro Romano) topped with a statue of the Virgin, balanced at the rear by an Egyptian obelisk placed there in 1587.

The vast nave with 40 ancient columns is part of the 5th-century build-ing, though the decorated pavement is medieval, as is the bell-tower (the tallest in Rome). Best of all are the 5th-century mosaics in the architrave (36 scenes from the Old Testament) and those on the triumphal arch above the altar. In the apse is Jacopo Torriti's mosaic the *Coronation of the Virgin* (1275). The coffered ceiling was commissioned by Alexander VI (1492–1503) and is thought to have been gilded using the first gold to reach Europe from the New World, a gift from Spain to the Spanish Borgia pope. The Cappella Sistina, built for Sixtus V (1585–90), is filled with precious marbles looted from Rome's ancient monuments. *Piazza di Santa Maria Maggiore. Bus: 16, 27, 70, 71, 93. Metro: Termini.*

SANTA MARIA SOPRA MINERVA,

see page 106.

Santa Maria del Popolo houses many fine paintings

The canopy and ceiling of Santa Maria Maggiore are a golden extravaganza

SANTA MARIA DI MONSERRATO

The 16th-century Spanish church in Rome, built to the designs of Antonio da Sangallo the Younger, contains the tombs of the Spanish Borgia pope Alexander VI and King Alfonso XIII of Spain. Also look out for Annibale Carracci's painting *S Diego di Alcala* in the first chapel to the right and Bernini's bust of Cardinal Pedro de Montoya in the room to the left of the choir.
Via di Monserrato, 15. Open: by special permission – apply to above address. Buses: 23, 41, 46, 62, 64, 65.

SANTA MARIA DELLA PACE, see page 111.

SANTA MARIA DEL POPOLO

Said to have been built on the site of Nero's tomb in 1099, the church is one of Rome's great artistic treasure-houses. In 1505 Bramante extended the apse; most of the interior work was directed later by Bernini, though the Cappella Chigi (second on the left) was designed by Raphael (1513) and has an altarpiece by Sebastiano del Piombo. Caravaggio's dramatic *Martyrdom of St Peter* and *Conversion of St Paul* (1601–2) in the Cappella Cerasi to the left of the high altar are generally considered the church's finest paintings. Behind the high altar are magnificent frescos (1508–9) by Pinturicchio .
Piazza del Popolo. Bus: 90, 90b, 95, 119. Metro: Flaminio.

> *[It is] composed of yards and yards of trailing red marble, like velvet in a draper's window, with a prowling lion below, looking like Oscar Wilde in a temper, and a snarling eagle above, and two naked cupids hanging the portrait of a long-nosed female in between ....*
>
> SEAN O'FAOLAIN, in Summer in Italy (1949) on the monument outside the Chigi Chapel in Santa Maria del Popolo.

Mosaics adorn the ancient façade of Santa Maria in Trastevere

SANTA MARIA IN TRASTEVERE

In the heart of Trastevere, this largely 12th-century building occupies a spot chosen by Pope Calixtus I in the 3rd century. A simple 12th-century bell-tower and façade are joined to Domenico Fontana's portico (1702). Mosaics on the façade depict Mary feeding the baby Jesus and 10 figures holding lamps. More lovely mosaics decorate the apse: the upper ones (1140) include Christ and the Virgin enthroned, and those in the lower apse, by Pietro Cavallini (1290), depict scenes from the life of the Virgin. The 22 nave columns come from the Terme di Caracalla (see page 91).
Piazza Santa Maria in Trastevere. Bus: 44, 56, 60, 75, 97, 170.

SANTA MARIA DELLA VITTORIA

Stendhal thought the interior of this church, built in 1610–12, looked like a boudoir, but it contains one of Bernini's most inspired works, the *Ecstasy of St Teresa* in the Cappella Cornaro (1644–7). At the centre, St Teresa of Avila (1515–82, mystic and refounder of the Carmelites) experiences a vision in which an angel brings her the love of God, symbolised by a spear aimed at her heart. Her smile has long been said to be one of the best in sculpture. The chapel encompasses a range of different worlds: heaven in the vault; the visionary world of the saint; the material world of the Cornaro family whose figures 'watch' from the sides; and the world of the dead represented by two skeletons in the pavement. Architecture, painting and sculpture are combined to produce illusionism at its greatest.
Via XX Settembre. Bus: 16, 36, 37, 60, 61, 62.

SANTA MARIA IN VALLICELLA
(also called Chiesa Nuova)

Located beside the Oratorio dei Filippini (see page 61), this church was begun in 1575 to replace the medieval Santa Maria in Vallicella and has been known as the Chiesa Nuova (New Church) ever since. Started by St Philip Neri's favourite architect, Matteo Città di Castello, the building was continued by Martino Longhi the Elder after 1582.

The Chiesa Nuova has one of the most complete and harmonious baroque

interiors in Rome, in spite of the fact that St Philip wanted it left unadorned. In the 1640s Pietro da Cortona frescoed the nave, dome and apse, and there are paintings (1606–87) by Rubens: *Madonna and Angels* in the centre of the high altar, *St Domitilla with St Nereus and St Achilleus* to the right of it and *St Gregory the Great with St Papianus and St Maurus* to the left.
Piazza della Chiesa Nuova. Bus: 46, 62, 64.

SAN PAOLO FUORI LE MURA (St Paul outside the Walls)

This ancient church is one of Rome's four patriarchal basilicas. Begun in the 4th century, it marks the spot where St Paul was buried after his execution in 67. Sadly it burned down in the 19th century and, although the church was faithfully reconstructed, the result is soulless and sterile.

San Paolo was once one of the treasure-houses of ancient Christendom

The reconstructed church and cloisters of San Paolo fuori le Mura

(in the 9th century Saracens looted 5 tonnes of gold and silver from it), and before the construction of St Peter's it was the biggest Christian basilica in the world. Only the 13th-century cloister evokes any sense of its great age. Do not miss Arnolfo di Cambio's altar canopy (1285) which miraculously survived the fire, and the nave mosaic showing all 265 popes from St Peter onwards. Below the altar is the tomb of St Paul which may or may not contain his bones (the Saracens looted this too). The mosaic on the main façade is 19th century.
Via Ostiense. Bus: 23, 93b, 170. Metro: San Paolo.

St Teresa in ecstasy, Bernini's magnificent sculpture

San Pietro

(St Peter's)

*T*he history of St Peter's in its present form begins with Bramante who, in the early 16th century, began a vast new domed building to replace the old basilica of Constantine (consecrated in 326), which itself replaced the ancient Circus of Nero. It took more than a century to complete – ample time for most of the great architects of the Renaissance and the baroque to contribute to its design and construction – and was finally consecrated in 1626.

Good and Bad Designs

Pope Julius II ordered work to start on a new St Peter's in 1506. The plan of Bramante's building was based on the Greek cross, a centralised plan inspired by his study of ancient Roman baths.

St Peter's is just one element of the busy, working Vatican City

However, Bramante died in 1514 and it was not until 1547 that Michelangelo took over the project. He simplified Bramante's plan, keeping a centralised design but increasing the scale tremendously and introducing giant Corinthian pilasters around the exterior. Michelangelo died in 1564, but by then much of the apse, the transepts and the

nave had already been completed. It was left to his pupil, Giacomo della Porta, to erect the dome in 1590 to Michelangelo's design. The entrance to Constantine's old basilica was still in use up to the early 17th century when Carlo Maderno, under a commission from Pope Paul V, destroyed it in lengthening the nave. At the same time his new façade ruined the view of the dome from the front, a mistake for which he has been vilified ever since.

Bernini's Contribution

Bernini was responsible for much of the decoration within. Beneath the dome, and forming the focus of the nave, is his huge **Baldacchino** which, with its barley-sugar columns, was cast from bronze stripped from the roof of the Pantheon. This extraordinary construction was unveiled by the Barberini Pope Urban VIII in 1633: notice the Barberini bees clambering all over it. The altar beneath it, dating from the pontificate of Clement VIII (1592–1605), is a plain slab of marble from the Forum of Nerva. It hovers above the well of the crypt in which the body of St Peter is reputedly buried. Behind the altar, in the tribune, is Bernini's **Cathedra**, a masterpiece of baroque theatricality. A halo of light illuminates the image of the Holy Spirit shown as a dove hovering above the Four Fathers of the Church.

Statues and Monuments

Michelangelo's beautiful *Pietà* stands in the first chapel to the right of the entrance, securely screened since it was attacked with an axe in 1972. Executed in 1499 when Michelangelo was only 24, it is one of his most moving works and the only sculpture he ever signed.

Soaring above the tomb of St Peter – Michelangelo's dome

At the end of the nave, on the right, is the 13th-century bronze statue of St Peter, attributed to Arnolfo di Cambio. Its foot, much kissed, is wearing away. To the left of the transept is Bernini's **Monument to Alexander VII** (1678): the Pope towers above the figures of Truth, Justice, Charity and Prudence. See also Canova's **Monument to the Stuarts** in the left aisle, behind the first pier, and the 18th-century tomb of Princess Clementina Sobieska, wife of Prince James Stewart, the 'Old Pretender', claimant to the throne of Great Britain.

From St Peter's (open: daily, 7am–7pm) it is possible to visit the Treasury (open: 9am–6pm; October to March, until 5pm; admission charge), the Vatican Grottoes (open: 7am–6pm; October to March, until 5pm), and the Dome (open: 8.00am–6pm; October to March, until 4.45pm; admission charge). Bus: 64 to Piazza San Pietro.

Santa Pudenziana is thought to occupy the site of a house visited by St Peter

SAN PIETRO IN MONTORIO, see page 115.

SAN PIETRO IN VINCOLI AND SANTA PRASSEDE, see page 113.

SANTA PUDENZIANA

This early Christian church contains a splendid 4th- to 5th-century apse mosaic depicting Christ surrounded by the Apostles dressed in togas. It is thought to have been constructed within baths built on the site of the house of a senator named Pudens, supposed father of Pudenziana and Prassede (see page 113). Pudenziana is frescoed in the pediment of the façade dressed as a Byzantine empress.
Via Urbana. Variable and restricted opening. Bus: 16, 70, 71, 93, 93b, 613. Metro: Cavour.

SANTA SABINA, see page 121.

SCALA SANTA AND SANCTA SANCTORUM

The Scala Santa (Holy Staircase), brought from Jerusalem by Constantine's mother St Helena, is reputed to be the very stairs which Christ ascended in Pontius Pilate's house during his trial. It is one of the most revered relics in Rome, and the devout climb its 28 steps on their knees to reach the Sancta Sanctorum (Holy of Holies) built by Pope Nicholas III in 1278 to house an image of Jesus said to have been painted by St Luke with the help of an angel.
Piazza di San Giovanni in Laterano 14. Bus: 4, 15, 16, 85, 87, 93. Metro: San Giovanni.

SCALINATA DELLA TRINITÀ DEI MONTI (The Spanish Steps)

Known as the Spanish Steps from the Piazza di Spagna at the foot, they were actually paid for by the French ambassador in 1723 and were once the haunt of painters and their models.

Bernini's original plan, with an equestrian statue of Louis XIV at the top of the steps, was rejected and the project

shelved until Clement VI commissioned Francesco de' Sanctis to complete it. *Bus 119. Metro: Spagna.*

TEATRO DI MARCELLO (Theatre of Marcellus)

A theatre for 20,000 people was begun by Julius Caesar and completed in 11BC by Augustus, who dedicated it to his nephew Marcellus. By the 4th century it was being plundered for stone, but because of its strategic position near the Tiber it was turned into a fortress in the Middle Ages. The building was turned into a palace in the 16th century, then in 1932 Mussolini cleared away a shambles of old houses and shops to reveal the ancient found-ations and double order of semi-columns. *Via del Teatro di Marcello. Bus: 57, 90, 90b, 92, 94.*

TERME DI CARACALLA (Baths of Caracalla)

The baths were begun in AD206 and completed by Caracalla in 217. Judging by the scale of the ruins and the large number of masterpieces of sculpture unearthed here in the 16th century, they must have been extraordinarily luxurious. *Viale di Terme di Caracalla 52 (tel: 575 8626). Open: Tuesday to Saturday, 9am–6pm (October to March, until 3pm); Sunday and Monday, 9am–1pm. Admission charge. Bus: 90, 93.*

TERME DI DIOCLEZIANO (Baths of Diocletian)

For an idea of the interior of Roman baths visit Santa Maria degli Angeli and the Museo Nazionale Romano, both within the 4th-century Baths of Diocletian. Originally, the complex covered over a hectare of ground between the present Piazza dei Cinquecento and Piazza della Repubblica and could accommodate over 3,000 people. The shape of an attached stadium can still be traced in the curve of two 19th-century buildings forming the southwestern perimeter of Piazza della Repubblica. *Piazza della Repubblica. Bus: 57, 65, 75, 170, 492. Metro: Repubblica, Termini.*

TRINITÀ DEI MONTI

Standing at the top of the Spanish Steps, the church of Trinità dei Monti is thought to be the work of Carlo Maderno. Richly endowed by successive French kings and cardinals, its principal treasures are works by Daniele da Volterra, notorious as the painter of clothes on to Michelangelo's nudes in the *Last Judgement* in the Sistine Chapel. *Bus: 119. Metro: Spagna.*

Right: the Spanish Steps
Left: in solitude, the Baths of Caracalla

THE PAPACY

The history of the modern papacy begins with Pope John XXIII (1958–63) who in 1958 summoned the Second Vatican Council in an effort to get the Church to put its house in order. The result was much-needed reform. Pope John asserted that the doctrines of the church are immutable but that the method of imparting them must change from generation to generation.

His successor, Pope Paul VI (1963–78), continued the process and, where John XXIII had taken only moderate steps to break out of the Vatican and reach the outside world, Paul VI went abroad and even welcomed to the Vatican heads of Communist countries. Despite his reforms, Paul VI is most remembered for his encyclical *Humanae Vitae,* confirming the Church's ban on artificial birth control.

John Paul I died just 33 days after his election in 1978. His successor was Karol Wojtyla who, as John Paul II, became the first non-Italian pope in 455 years. Such a choice – a man from a nation under Communist rule – was an astonishing break with tradition.

Pope John Paul II presides over the Vatican, tiniest of states yet controlling a religious community of over 739 million or 18 per cent of the world's population. The most striking features of his pontificate are his triumphal progresses around the globe, demonstrating the physical presence of the papacy; his disapproval of doctrinal innovations; and his conservative attitude to questions of discipline and morals. His humanity, accessibility and understanding of human nature are contrasted with his rigid views on such controversial issues as clerical

IN THE MODERN WORLD

marriage, the admission of women to the priesthood, divorce, contraception, abortion and homosexuality – issues which, it is claimed, are driving Catholics from the Church.

Far left: the Pope in St Peter's, saying Mass at Christmas
Centre: Mass at Easter, in the Piazza
Above: the Pope and the Faithful in an open-air audience chamber

Vaticano and the Musei Vaticani

(The Vatican and Vatican Museums)

*P*erhaps more than for anything else, the Vatican Museums are famous for their collections of Greek and Roman sculpture. Pope Julius II began to form this collection in the 16th century, but it was not until 200 years later that Clement XI and his successors conceived the idea of a museum proper. Under Benedict XIV the first of the Vatican Museums, dedicated to Christian antiquities, was opened (1756) in the Vatican Library.

Since then the museum complex has grown immeasurably and is today the world's greatest collection of western art. It is housed in the papal palace built

1. Ufficio Informazioni
2. Ufficio Postale
3. Arco delle Campane
4. Portone di Bronzo
5. Ufficio Scavi
6. Museo Storico Artistico
7. Giardino Quadrato
8. Fontana dell'Aquilone
9. Fontana del Sacramento

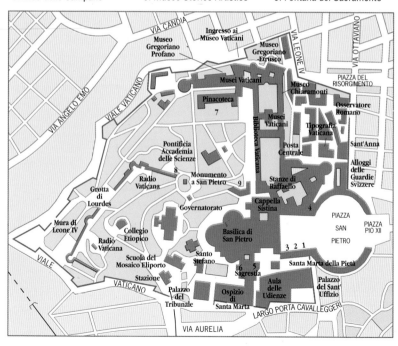

Above: the Vatican Museum complex is one of the finest collections of art in the world but also one of the largest

during the Renaissance for Sixtus IV, Innocent VIII and Julius II. Bramante designed a part of it, and there were significant additions in the 18th century. The complex also houses the Cappella Sistina (Sistine Chapel) and the Stanze di Raffaello (Raphael Rooms), a series of chambers frescoed by Raphael.

A visit to the museums can be daunting, to say the least. However, the museum helpfully suggests four itineraries around the collections, each one colour-coded. They vary in length from 90 minutes to five hours. Should you wish to see the Sistine Chapel or the Raphael Rooms only, go as early as possible as they get very crowded. Both are a 20- to 30-minute walk through the museum from its entrance.

Entrance: Viale Vaticano (tel: 69883332). Open: October to June, Monday to Saturday, 9am–2pm; Holy Week and July to September, Monday to Friday, 9am–5pm; Saturday, 9am–2pm. Closed religious holidays and Sunday throughout the year except last Sunday of every month (winter, 9am–2pm; summer, 9am–5pm). The ticket office closes 1 hour before closing time. Admission charge, but free on last Sunday of month.

To visit the Vatican Gardens, book two days in advance: November to February, Tuesday, Thursday and Saturday, 10am; March to October, Tuesday, Friday and Saturday, 10am. Admission charge. Book at information office (tel: 69884466), right of St Peter's entrance. Bus: 64 (to Piazza San Pietro), 23, 81, 492 (to Piazza del Risorgimento). Metro: Ottaviano.

The highlights of each of the museum's sections are described below and on pages 98–102. The sights are arranged geographically.

MUSEO GREGORIANO EGIZIO

The Egyptian collection contains the finds from 19th- and 20th-century excavations (mummies, sarcophagi, statues, funerary artefacts) and, most interesting, the Egyptian-style Roman statuary (Room III) from the Villa Adriana (see page 128).

MUSEO CHIARAMONTI AND MUSEO PIO-CLEMENTINO

These two sections contain the Vatican's huge collection of classical

FOR FOOTSORE VISITORS

FOR FOOTSORE VISITORS
Had enough? Weary? Well, do not be ashamed: you are in good company. Anton Chekhov, writing to a friend in Moscow after his Vatican visit, said: 'Sauntering around the Vatican, I wilted from exhaustion, and when I got home, my legs felt as if they were made out of cotton'.

sculpture. The less interesting Chiaramonti Museum has many portrait busts, as well as a famous statue of Augustus. The Museo Pio-Clementino's treasures include the *Apoxyomenos* , a 1st-century Roman copy of a Greek original portraying an athlete scraping his body (Room X) and the *Apollo Belvedere* (AD130), another Roman copy, in Room VIII. Next to the *Apollo* is the *Laocoön* group (50BC) described by Pliny the Elder. It was dug from the ruins of the Domus Aurea (see page 29) and wrongly reassembled by Michelangelo. The *Belvedere Torso* (1st century AD), an object of veneration for sculptors from the Renaissance to Rodin, is in Room III. The Sala degli Animale is filled with carved animals, many of them heavily restored. From the Villa Adriana (see page 128) came the Candelabri Barberini, original 2nd-century lamps.

MUSEO GREGORIANO-ETRUSCO

The Etruscan section (18 rooms) contains an astonishing collection of artefacts taken

Laocoön and his sons (c.25BC), in the Museo Pio-Clementino

from sites including Cerveteri (see page 125) and Tarquinia (see page 128). Do not miss Room II where furniture and gold artefacts found in the 7th-century BC Tomba di Regolini-Galassi at Cerveteri are displayed. Other rooms contain early sculpture, funeral *stelae*, pottery and votive offerings. Room XII contains a distinguished collection of Greek sculpture, a strong influence on Etruscan culture.

SALA DELLA BIGA

Visit this room to see the remains of a 1st-century BC two-horsed chariot (see page161 for a description of chariot racing). Until the 18th century it was used as part of the episcopal throne in the church of San Marco (see page 79).

GALLERIA DEI CANDELABRI

The first of three galleries built by Bramante to link different areas of the palace, this contains pairs of marble candlesticks from the imperial era of ancient Rome, as well as a quantity of marble statuary.

GALLERIA DEGLI ARAZZI

This gallery takes its name from the tapestries *(arazzi)* contained in it. Ten 16th-century Brussels tapestries, based on cartoons from Raphael's workshop, illustrate stories from the life of Christ. On the right wall are tapestries recording events from the life of the Barberini pope, Urban VIII, commissioned in his honour in the 17th century by his nephew .

GALLERIA DELLE CARTE GEOGRAFICHE

The Map Gallery has 40 panels painted on its walls in the 16th century. Each one depicts a region, island or particular territory of Italy.

Papal territories: the Map Gallery

GALLERIA DI PIO V

Pius V's Gallery contains precious 15th-century tapestries from Tournai illustrating the Baptism and Passion of Christ.

SALA DI SOBIESKI

This room holds a huge painting of Jan III Sobieski (king of Poland), defeating the Turks at Vienna (1683).

SALA DELLA CONCEZIONE

This room, decorated with frescos, is devoted to Pius IX's proclamation on the dogma of the Immaculate Conception (1854). It also contains Michelangelo's model for the dome of St Peter's.

STANZE DI RAFFAELLO

Julius II balked at the idea of occupying the apartments used by his unsavoury Borgia predecessor, Alexander VI, and in 1509 commissioned Raphael to redecorate a suite of four small rooms for his own use. By 1520, the year of Raphael's death, only three of the rooms were complete and not all of them were wholly painted by the master. Nevertheless, this is one of the greatest cycles of fresco painting from the High Renaissance, even if great works by earlier masters of Renaissance painting, Perugino and Piero della Francesca among them, were obliterated in the process.

An ageing Raphael had *carte blanche* to decorate four rooms of the Papal Suite for Pope Julius II

Room I: Stanza dell'Incendio del Borgo (1514–17)

The Room of the Fire in the Borgo was the last room Raphael worked on. Much of the decoration was carried out by Giulio Romano, Giovanni Penni and Giovanni da Udine, and the patron was by that time Julius II's successor, Leo X. The subjects celebrate the virtues of Pope Leo's previous namesakes: the *Coronation of Charlemagne in St Peter's* (by Leo III; old St Peter's is depicted); the *Oath of Leo III*; the *Battle of Ostia*, which recalls an attempted invasion by the Saracens in 848 repulsed by Leo IV; and the *Fire in the Borgo*, depicting the fire of 847 extinguished by Leo IV with the sign of the cross.

Room II: Stanza della Segnatura (1508–11)

The first to be completed, this room was executed almost entirely by Raphael. The name derives from the papal bulls that were signed here *(segnatura* means signature). Three themes are illustrated : Truth, Goodness and Beauty. Truth is celebrated in its two aspects: Theology (spiritual truth) and Philosophy (rational truth). On the long wall (behind you on entry), the *Disputation of the Holy Sacrament* exalts Theology, celebrating the triumph of religious faith. In the lower section the earthly domain includes the pope, the clergy and the faithful, while the upper part shows heaven with God, Christ and the Virgin. On the wall opposite is the *School of Athens* representing the triumph of Philosophy through the depiction of a debate between Plato and Aristotle, searchers for truth. *Parnassus,* above the window, celebrates Beauty: Apollo is surrounded by the Muses, poets and writers. Opposite, in the lunette,

Art pilgrims fill the Stanze di Raffaello

Goodness is the theme, with canon and civil law glorified through allegorical representations of Prudence, Fortitude and Temperance. In the vaults are personifications of Poetry, Philosophy, Justice and Theology by Perugino (Raphael's teacher).

Room III: Stanza d'Eliodoro (1512–14)
The name of this room refers to the main fresco on the right: *The Expulsion of Heliodorus from the Temple*. It illustrates the story of the thief Heliodorus, struck down as he tried to make off with the treasure from the Temple of Jerusalem. It is seen as a justification of Julius II's attempts to drive foreign armies off Italian soil. In *Leo I Repulsing Attila* the central figure bears the likeness of Leo X, while Julius II appears in *The Mass at Bolsena*, borne on a litter by the Swiss

Guards. Over the window, *The Liberation of St Peter* commemorates St Peter's miraculous escape from prison.

Room IV: Sala di Costantino (1517–24)
None of the frescos in this room is by Raphael though one, *Constantine's Victory over Maxentius*, is based on his drawings. The work was completed in 1526 by Giulio Romano, Giovanni Penni and Raffaellino del Colle, and its theme is the triumph of Christianity over paganism, seen through events from the life of Constantine the Great.

Cappella di Nicolo V
The Chapel of Nicholas V is decorated with frescos by Fra Angelico (1447–51) depicting scenes from the lives of St Stephen and St Lawrence.

APPARTAMENTO BORGIA

The decoration (1492–5) by Pinturicchio of the rooms used by Alexander VI and his ignoble family contrasts vividly with the unlovely goings-on in the rooms during the Borgia occupation.

BIBLIOTECA APOSTOLICA VATICANA

This section contains a small but important part of the illustrious Vatican Library; the manuscripts written by the likes of Michelangelo and St Thomas Aquinas are breathtaking.

COLLEZIONE DI ARTE RELIGIOSA MODERNA

In 55 rooms are 800 works of recent religious art, including contributions from Dali, Matisse, Munch, Picasso and Moore.

CAPPELLA SISTINA (Sistine Chapel)

Frescos, acres of them, make an unlovely building an object of sheer delight and fascination. Behind the altar is Michelangelo's *Last Judgement*, and in the vaults his scenes from the Old Testament and his classical Sibyls. The chapel was built for Pope Sixtus IV (hence its name) in 1475–80, and the side walls were decorated by a variety of leading Renaissance painters. Look for Perugino's *Handing over the Keys to St Peter* (fifth from *Last Judgement*, right), Signorelli's *Death of Moses* (sixth from *Last Judgement*, left) , Botticelli's *Punishment of the Rebels* (fifth from *Last Judgement*, left) and his *Temptations of Christ* (second from *Last Judgement*, left). There are also paintings by Ghirlandaio, Rosselli, Pinturicchio and di Cosimo.

The Last Judgement

This huge fresco is considered to be Michelangelo's masterpiece. It was commissioned by Pope Paul III and completed in 1541, having taken seven years. At top centre Christ the Judge raises the dead, beckoning the rightous (left) to Paradise and consigning the wicked (right) to Hell. The work was commissioned in the wake of the

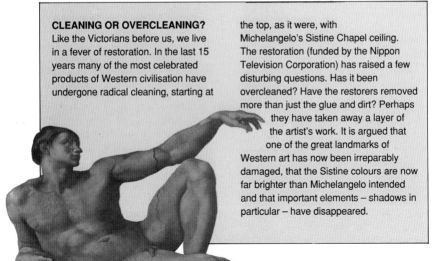

CLEANING OR OVERCLEANING?
Like the Victorians before us, we live in a fever of restoration. In the last 15 years many of the most celebrated products of Western civilisation have undergone radical cleaning, starting at the top, as it were, with Michelangelo's Sistine Chapel ceiling. The restoration (funded by the Nippon Television Corporation) has raised a few disturbing questions. Has it been overcleaned? Have the restorers removed more than just the glue and dirt? Perhaps they have taken away a layer of the artist's work. It is argued that one of the great landmarks of Western art has now been irreparably damaged, that the Sistine colours are now far brighter than Michelangelo intended and that important elements – shadows in particular – have disappeared.

The rejuvenated ceiling of the Sistine Chapel

Reformation and the powerful theme is rendered with terrifying force and unbridled emotion by Michelangelo. Surrounding Christ are the saints and the Virgin, who cowers behind him, and below is Charon, the ferryman of the dead, rowing towards Hades and Minos, judge of the infernal world. The power of this work has as much to do with the artist's style as with the subject matter. Dark and sombre, it depicts a pitiless God exacting a terrible, almost apocalyptic vengeance on the wicked.

In 1564 Daniele da Volterra was commanded to cover up the figures' nudity, by then considered offensive. Some of his work has since been removed.

The Ceiling

Lying flat on his back on a scaffold, Michelangelo worked on the chapel's ceiling for four years (1508–12), singlehandedly painting what his biographer Condivi called a wonder of the world. Its subject was scenes from the Old Testament. *The Creation of Adam* is familiar to most people, as are the *Creation of Sun and Moon* and the *Original Sin* panels. Michelangelo painted *trompe l'oeil* architecture to give definition to the vaults and, between the great scenes, the writhing, athletic male nudes known as the *ignudi*. In the lunettes above the windows he depicted the forerunners of Christ and, in between these, the Sibyls and Prophets.

The Salone delle Prospettive in the Villa Farnesina

PINACOTECA

This is the Vatican's vast picture gallery and it contains a bit of everything spread over its 18 rooms. Room VIII is devoted to work by Raphael: his *Transfiguration* ,

---

AGOSTINO CHIGI

The wealthy banker for whom the Villa Farnesina was built was without shame. The pagan scheme of decoration in the Loggia of the Villa Farnesina, telling the story of Cupid and Psyche, commemorated his marriage to his mistress, at which his friend Pope Leo X officiated, having already baptised their four illegitimate children. Once the gardens of the Villa led down to the Tiber. It is said that Chigi, eager to impress his guests with his wealth, habitually threw his gold plate into the river after dinner, only to have it fished out of the net concealed beneath the water once the revellers had departed.

Coronation of the Virgin and *Madonna of Foligno* are all here, as well as the tapestries he designed for the Sistine Chapel. In Room IX is Leonardo da Vinci's *St Jerome*. Elsewhere are paintings by Bellini, Caravaggio, Thomas Lawrence, Poussin, Giulio Romano, Van Dyck and Veronese.

MUSEO GREGORIANO PROFANO

Here you will see 'profane' (pagan) art. This consists mainly of sculpture, both Greek and Roman originals and Roman copies of Greek originals.

MUSEO PIO CRISTIANO

This museum traces the history of Christianity, and much of its contents (including a formidable collection of sarcophagi) came from the excavations of the catacombs.

MUSEO MISSIONARIO ETNOLOGICO

Crammed into the basement is an enormous collection of artefacts from other religions and cults worldwide, some of it dating from the pre-Christian era, as well as examples of Christian art from countries with missions.

MUSEO STORICO

All the paraphernalia of the Papal State is here – papal carriages, flags and banners.

VILLAS

VILLA FARNESINA

In Trastevere, the riverside Villa Farnesina is filled with artistic treasures of the Renaissance. It merits a good morning's viewing.

Occupying the site of Caesar's country villa, it was built in 1508 for a hugely rich Sienese banker, Agostino Chigi, then bought by the Farnese in 1577 – hence the name. The architect was Baldassare Peruzzi, a brilliant designer who had been assistant to Bramante and who took over from Raphael as Head of Works at St Peter's in 1520 on the latter's death. Chigi's intention was to create a retreat, somewhere he could entertain in lavish style away from the noise and dirt of the city. Essentially frivolous, this is how the building and its decorations should be 'read'.

The interior decorations date from 1510 to 1519. The Loggia of Cupid and Psyche (1517), a lyrical *trompe-l'œil* 'bower', was designed by Raphael but most of the work was carried out by assistants, notably Giulio Romano and Giovanni da Udine. The real authorship of these frescos has always been the subject of much argument. Even before work stopped in 1517, the rumour went round that Raphael was so sated by his mistress, La Fornarina, that he was unable to paint. The bulbous fruit and

vegetables are suggestive of sex and fertility. Now glazed in, it was once an open garden 'room'. *Galatea*, in the adjacent Room of Galatea, is by Raphael alone, though the Signs of the Zodiac are Peruzzi's work. The Salone delle Prospettive is also Peruzzi's: the walls of this room were decorated with illusionistic views of the Roman skyline, even though the villa was built as a retreat from the city. Next door, in Chigi's bedroom, are scenes from the nuptials of Alexander the Great and Roxana by Sodoma.

Via della Lungara 230 (tel: 68 80 17 67).
Open: Monday to Saturday, 9am–1pm.
Bus: 23, 65, 280.

VILLA MEDICI, see page 111.

'Al fresco' bower: the Loggia of Cupid and Psyche, Villa Farnesina

Roman Monuments

Many of the monuments of ancient Rome form part of the fabric of the modern city. Some have been preserved in the structure of newer buildings, others revealed as later accretions were cleared away. This walk identifies a selection. *Allow 3 hours.*

Start in the Via di Ripetta.

1 ARA PACIS AUGUSTAE

Augustus' Altar of Peace, one of the great works of Roman sculpture, was commissioned by the Senate in 13BC to celebrate the Augustan peace. It was reconstructed here in 1938. *Cross Via di Ripetta.*

2 MAUSOLEO DI AUGUSTO

Augustus' Mausoleum (28BC) has been at different times stronghold, bull-ring, circus and concert hall. It originally contained four concentric circles of corridors.

Ara Pacis – Open: Tuesday to Saturday, 9am–1.30pm, Sunday 9am–1pm (April to September, Tuesday and Saturday, also 4–7pm). Admission charge.
Museo Barracco – Corso Vittorio Emanuele 168 (tel: 68 80 6848). Open: Tuesday to Sunday, 9am–1.30pm (Tuesday and Thursday, also 5–8pm). Admission charge.
Pantheon – Tel: 68 30 0230. Open: Monday to Saturday, 9am–6pm (until 5pm October to March), Sunday, 9am–1pm.

Continue south, down Via della Scrofa, turning right into Via dell'Orso. Take the first left, behind Sant'Agostino, and continue to Piazza dei Cinque Terre.

3 PIAZZA NAVONA, see page 111.

From the southwestern end of the piazza turn into Piazza San Pantaleo. Go left to Corso Vittorio Emanuele II.

4 MUSEO BARRACCO

This tiny museum contains a collection of Assyrian, Egyptian, early Greek and Roman sculpture assembled in the 19th century by Baron Barracco.
Continue east along Corso Vittorio Emanuele II, then turn right into Via dei Chiavari. In the Largo dei Pallaro branch right and continue into Via Grotta Pinta

5 TEATRO DI POMPEI

The shape of the vanished Theatre of Pompey's auditorium, where Caesar was assassinated, survives in the curved structure of the Palazzo Righetti.
From Piazza dei Sartiri, go right then first left down Vicolo dei Chidaroli, continuing along Via di Sant'Anna.

6 LARGO DI TORRE ARGENTINA

In 1926 excavations revealed some of Rome's earliest buildings including four Republican temples.
Cross Corso Vittorio Emanuele II and continue down Via di Torre Argentina.

7 PANTHEON (SANTA MARIA AD MARTYRES)

Now a church, the Pantheon was built over 18 centuries ago by Hadrian, who dedicated it to the 12 Olympian gods of ancient Greece. The bejewelled statue of Venus, long gone, wore in its ear one half of the famous large pearl whose other half was dissolved and drunk by Cleopatra. A

The Pantheon

simple brick drum is topped by a shallow dome (span 43m) pierced by an *oculus.* Open to the elements, this allowed greater 'interaction' between gods and the faithful. The proportions within are perfect: floor to ceiling height equals the dome's diameter while the side walls are half the height of the dome. Apart from the tombs and altars, the building's interior is entirely original.
Exit Piazza della Rotonda by Via dei Bastini, and continue to Piazza di Pietra..

8 TEMPIO DI ADRIANO

All that remains of the Temple of Hadrian (dedicated in AD145 by Hadrian's successor Antoninus Pius) are 11 marble Corinthian columns.
At its northeastern corner, the piazza opens to Piazza Colonna.

9 COLONNA DI MARCO AURELIO

This column celebrates Marcus Aurelius' triumphs in the Danube region. A continuous spiralling relief chronicles the events and contains a wealth of detail on contemporary dress, and military and social life.
To return to the Ara Pacis, continue north down the Via del Corso for about 1km, turning left at the Via Ara Pacis.

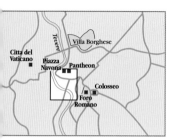

Renaissance Rome

Some of the key painters, architects and sculptors of the Renaissance were drawn to Rome under the patronage of the popes. Their work can be seen at sites all over the city. *Allow about 3 hours.*

Start at Piazza della Minerva.

1 SANTA MARIA SOPRA MINERVA

The church, built by the Dominicans in about 1280, stands on the site of the former Temple of Isis. It contains a series of early Renaissance chapels, including the Cappella Carafa (right

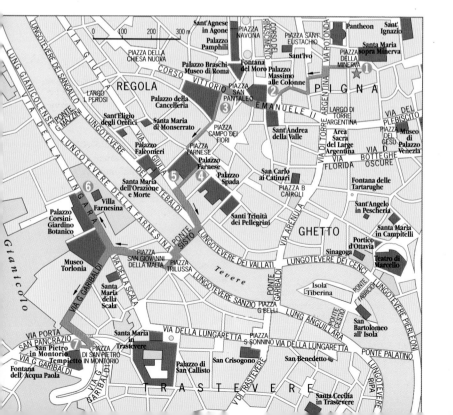

transept) with Filippino Lippi's magnificent fresco *The Assumption of Our Lady* (1488–93). To the left of the high altar is Michelangelo's statue of the Risen Christ (1519–20). In the crypt lie the remains of Italy's patron saint, Santa Caterina da Siena, while the choir contains the tombs of the Medici popes Leo X and Clement VII.
From Piazza della Minerva go along Via di Santa Chiara and left into Via di Torre Argentina. At Via dei Navi go right, then left into Via Monterone, and continue until the junction between Corso Vittorio Emanuele II and Corso del Rinascimento.

2 PALAZZO MASSIMO ALLE COLONNE

Baldassare Peruzzi (1532–6), one of the most accomplished architects of the High Renaissance working in Rome, designed this palace. His flouting of architectural convention produced a spirited building, nowhere better than in the curved façade following the line of the old Via Papale (replaced by the Corso).
Continue west along the Corso Vittorio Emanuele II. From Piazza San Pantaleo cross to Piazza della Cancelleria.

3 PALAZZO DELLA CANCELLERIA

An imposing Renaissance building, this was long thought to have been the work of Bramante but Andrea Bregna is now credited with its design. It housed Napoleon's court (1810), the Italian parliament (1848) and is today papal offices.
From Piazza della Cancelleria, continue through Piazza Campo dei Fiori and exit from Via dei Baullari into Piazza Farnese.

4 PALAZZO FARNESE, see page 66
Behind the palace is the Via Giulia.

> **Palazzo Massimo alle Colonne** – Open: 16 March only, 7am–1pm.
> **Palazzo della Cancelleria** – Entry by permit only.
> **Tempietto** – Open: daily, 9am–noon and 4–6pm.

5 VIA GIULIA

This kilometre-long street created by Bramante is named after Julius II, who commissioned it early in the 16th century. It was to have been the key element of a grand new approach to the Vatican, never completed.

Going south, cross Ponte Sisto and, beyond the Acqua Paolo in Piazza Trilussa, continue right into Piazza San Giovanni della Malta. Bear right and continue along Via della Lungara.

6 VILLA FARNESINA, see page 103.
Backtracking down Via della Lungara, go right, up Via G Garibaldi, and continue up the hill to Piazza di San Pietro in Montorio.

7 TEMPIETTO

In the courtyard to the right of San Pietro in Montorio is Bramante's *Tempietto* ('little temple') built on the traditional site of St Peter's execution. Considered the first great monument of the High Renaissance (1502), this domed cylinder surrounded by a Tuscan Doric colonnade came closer than any other building to the spirit of antiquity. The scale is tiny but the proportions are a masterly evocation of the majesty of ancient Rome, which the Renaissance sought to emulate.
Retrace your steps to the Villa Farnesina. On its river side, buses go to the Largo di Torre Argentina from where it is a short walk back to Piazza della Minerva.

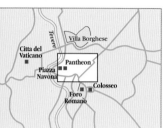

Baroque Rome

The baroque is Rome's most characteristic architectural style. *Allow 3 hours.*

Begin in Piazza Navona.

1 PIAZZA NAVONA, see page 111.
Leave the piazza by Corsia Agonale, turn left into Corso del Rinascimento, then first right down Via del Salvatore.

2 SAN LUIGI DEI FRANCESI
The principal baroque feature of the French national church (founded 1518) is provided by Caravaggio's dramatic paintings in the Cappella Contarelli (5th chapel, left) depicting scenes from the life of St Matthew. Caravaggio's paintings are characterised by vivid realism and strong contrasts of light and shade and powerful sensuality (see page 63).
Going right from the church, continue to Piazza Sant'Eustachio.

3 SANT'IVO ALLA SAPIENZA
The Sapienza was the seat of the old University of Rome from

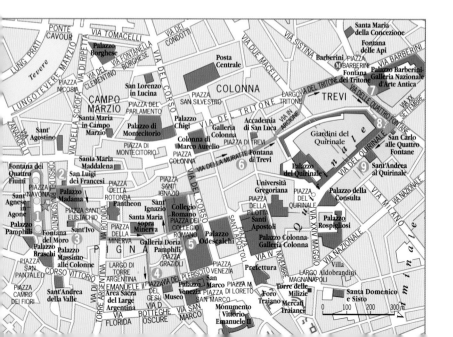

the 15th century to 1935. Dominating its internal courtyard (by Giacomo della Porta) is Borromini's idiosyncratic church of Sant'Ivo (1642–60). The 'sculpted' feel of this building, particularly the play of convex and concave surfaces on the façade facing the courtyard, is a virtuoso performance, marking Borromini as one of the greatest baroque designers.
Continue on through Piazza della Minerva then right, down the Via del Gesù.

4 GESÙ
This church was designed by Vignola for Cardinal Alessandro Farnese who was said to have owned the three most beautiful things in Rome: his family palace (see page 66), his daughter and the Gesù. The Gesù is the epitome of Counter-Reformation style (see page 80/81). Its baroque interior seems to hold this message for the faithful: a hefty dose of spirituality in this life will be rewarded by heavenly pleasures in the next. As if to suggest this Il Baciccia's *Triumph of the Name of Jesus* (1670–83) glorifies the Faith by its exquisitely illusory effects and theatrical intensity, which heighten the senses and so bring the viewer 'closer' to God.
Cross Corso Vittorio Emanuele II and enter Piazza del Collegio Romano via Piazza Grazioli.

5 GALLERIA DORIA PAMPHILI, see page 52.
From Piazza Collegio Romano, enter Via Sant'Ignazio and continue through Piazza Sant'Ignazio to Via del Corso. On the right the Via della Muratte leads to Piazza di Trevi.

6 FONTANA DI TREVI, see page 43.
Follow the Via in Arcione to the Via del Tritone. From the Piazza Barberini, proceed right along the Via delle Quattro Fontane.

The Trevi Fountain

7 GALLERIA NAZIONALE D'ARTE ANTICA – PALAZZO BARBERINI,
see page 52.
At the gallery gates, go left and continue to the junction of Via delle Quattro Fontane and Via del Quirinale.

8 SAN CARLO ALLE QUATTRO FONTANE
Also known as San Carlino, this church was Borromini's first independent commission (for the Spanish Order of Discalced Trinitarians) and is a masterly solution for such a small site. With hardly a right angle in sight, its interior is a triumph of convexities and concavities, the drama increased rather than diminished by the almost total absence of colour.
Continue left down Via del Quirinale.

9 SANT'ANDREA AL QUIRINALE
Complementing Borromini's San Carlino, Bernini's church is much less frenetic, though on an equally constricted site. Designed in 1658, it was built for Cardinal Camillo Pamphili, the nephew of Pope Innocent X.
Buses in the nearby Via Nazionale go direct to the Largo di Torre Argentina and Corso Vittorio Emanuele II, from where a short walk takes you back to Piazza Navona.

Pincio to Santa Maria della Pace

This is an easy walk that cuts through the centre of town, passing shops, cafés and restaurants. *Allow a morning at a slow, steady pace.*

Begin on Monte Pincio (Pincio Hill) overlooking Rome.

1 PINCIO, see page 119
A steep ramp, on the left side of the terrace, descends to Viale Trinità dei Monti.

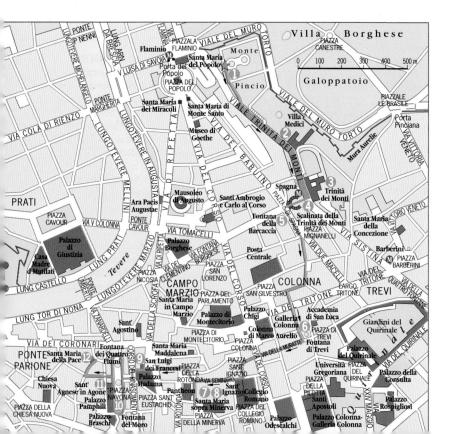

2 VILLA MEDICI

Originally Medici property, the villa now houses the French Academy. Past academicians include the painters Fragonard, Boucher and Ingres and the composers Berlioz and Debussy.
Continue along Viale Trinità dei Monti.

3 TRINITÀ DEI MONTI, see page 91.

4 SCALINATA DELLA TRINITÀ DEI MONTI (The Spanish Steps), see page 90.

5 FONTANA DELLA BARCACCIA, see page 42.

Proceed south past Piazza Mignanelli and along Via di Propaganda. Cross the Via del Tritone and continue straight ahead until you enter Piazza di Trevi.

6 FONTANA DI TREVI, see page 43.

Exit from the piazza down Via della Muratte, cross Via del Corso and continue down Via del Seminario to Piazza della Rotonda.

7 PANTHEON, see page 105.

Go south into Piazza della Minerva.

8 SANTA MARIA SOPRA MINERVA, see page 106.

Return to Piazza della Rotonda and take the northwest exit into Via del Salvatore. Proceed west towards Piazza San Luigi dei Francesi.

9 SAN LUIGI DEI FRANCESI, see page 108.

From Via del Salvatore, continue west, then cross Corso del Rinascimento.

10 PIAZZA NAVONA

Theatrical display is the hallmark of this piazza, deriving from the Pamphili pope Innocent X's decision in the 17th century to make it the 'family square' and a fitting memorial to his pontificate. Bernini's great Fontana dei Quattro Fiumi (see page 43) is at its centre and Sant'Agnese in Agone, next door to the Palazzo Pamphili (now the Brazilian embassy), dominates it from the west. Water festivals used to take place here in summer, when the fountains' drainage outlets were stopped up so that the piazza flooded.

The elongated Piazza Navona follows the outline of Domitian's Circus Agonalis, a 1st-century AD athletics stadium: the square's name derives from 'n'Agona', a corruption of Agonalis. It remained virtually unchanged as an arena for jousting and sports until Sixtus IV (1471–84) moved the market here from the Capitoline. The obelisk at its centre came from the Circo di Massenzio (see p117).

11 SANT'AGNESE IN AGONE

Completed in 1657 by Borromini, Bernini and Carlo Rainaldi, this church covers the site of St Agnes's martyrdom (see page 73). 'In Agone' is another corruption of 'Agonalis' (see above). The saint's skull is in the chapel to the left of the altar, and the Pamphili tombs, including that of Innocent X, are in the crypt.
Leave the piazza on its west side and cross Via di Santa Maria dell' Anima to reach Vicolo della Pace.

12 SANTA MARIA DELLA PACE

Hidden among the narrow streets of medieval Rome is this church built by Sixtus IV and restored for Alexander VII (1656–7) by Pietro da Cortona. Inside, in the Cappella Chigi, are Raphael's *Sibyls* (1514). The adjacent cloisters by Bramante (1500–4) are among his finest creations.
Bus 119 connects the north end of Piazza Navona with Piazza del Popolo (directly below the Pincio).

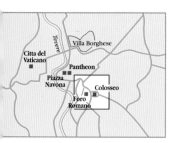

Saints and Martyrs

For the early Christians Rome was a most unhealthy place, and this walk uncovers some of its horrors. Wear comfortable shoes. *Allow a day (with a break for lunch).*

Approach San Pietro in Carcere from the Via dei Fori Imperiali.

1 CARCERE MAMERTINO

The Mamertine Prison was later consecrated as San Pietro in Carcere and now lies beneath the 16th-century church of San

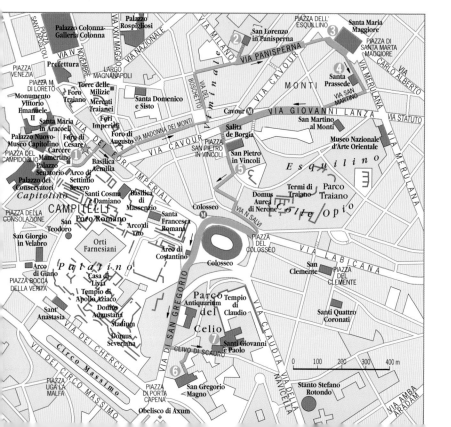

Giuseppe dei Falegnami (enter via the steps in the church porch). St Peter was held here by Nero before his crucifixion in AD67: the lower cell, the Tullianum contains the column to which he was secured. This cell was the scene of executions, and corpses were disposed of through the hole in the floor which led to the Cloaca Maxima sewer.

Cross Via dei Fori Imperiali and, continuing up Via Madonna dei Monti, turn left at Via del Boschetto then right into Via Panisperna.

2 SAN LORENZO IN PANISPERNA

This church on the Viminal is believed to have been built in the 6th century (restored in the 16th century) on the site of St Lawrence's martyrdom. He was roasted on a gridiron, a relic of which is kept here.

Continue along Via Panisperna and Via Santa Maria Maggiore.

3 SANTA MARIA MAGGIORE, see page 84.

From the main entrance on Piazza Santa Maria Maggiore, go down Via di Santa Prassede just to the right.

4 SANTA PRASSEDE

St Prassede was declared invalid in 1969: she and her sister Pudenziana (see page 90) were an invention, supposedly daughters of one Pudens, a friend of St Paul. The church, founded in the 9th century, is decorated with magnificent early mosaics, particularly in the Capella di San Zeno.

At the bottom of Via di Santa Prassede go right down Via San Martino and into Via Giovanni Lanza. Halfway down the Via Cavour ascend steps, the Salita dei Borgia, to Piazza San Pietro in Vincoli.

Carcere Mamertino – Open: daily, April to September, 9am–12.30pm and 2.30–6pm; October to March, 9am–noon and 2–5pm. Donation expected.

---

5 SAN PIETRO IN VINCOLI

The church of St Peter in Chains was built by Sixtus III (432–40) to house the chains that held St Peter prisoner in Jerusalem and Rome (kept in a casket beneath the high altar). Rebuilt by Sixtus IV (1471–84), the church also contains Michelangelo's unfinished tomb of Pope Julius II with its famous statue of Moses.

Leaving the church, go left and continue down Via Eudosiana towards Via N Salvi. Skirt the Colosseum and proceed down Via di San Gregorio.

6 SAN GREGORIO MAGNO

The church was founded by St Gregory the Great in 575 and restored in the 17th century. In the right-hand aisle St Gregory's chapel contains his episcopal throne (a 1st-century BC Roman carved marble seat) and his stone 'bed'.

Proceed up Clivo di Scauro.

7 SANTI GIOVANNI E PAOLO

This church is dedicated to two Roman soldiers, John and Paul, beheaded in AD362 for refusing the call to arms of the pagan Emperor Julian the Apostate. It was built in the 4th century and much remodelled in the 18th. A tomb slab in the nave marks the martyrs' burial place, while their relics are in an urn under the high altar.

Take bus 15 in Via di San Gregorio; change to bus 94 in Piazza Bocca della Verità, alighting in Piazza Venezia.

Piazza Campo dei Fiori to Fontana di Acqua Paola

This pleasant walk includes a market, churches, a palace interior including an art gallery, and an important fountain. *Allow no less than 3 hours. Break for lunch in Trastevere.*

Start in Piazza Campo dei Fiori.

1 **PIAZZA CAMPO DEI FIORI,** see page 144.
Via dei Baullari leads into Piazza Farnese.

2 **PALAZZO FARNESE,** see page 66.
Proceed along Via Capo di Ferro, left.

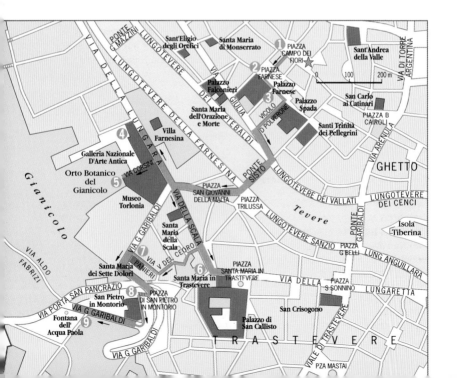

3 PALAZZO SPADA

The palace contains important paintings – collected in the 17th century by Cardinal Bernardino Spada – by Reni, Guercino, Rubens, Titian and Dürer. Notice the striking exterior: four storeys are adorned with exuberant stuccos (1556–60), inscriptions and figures of Roman heroes. The courtyard is similarly festooned. The palace was bought in 1632 by Spada, who remodelled it. A false perspective colonnade (1653) opens from the courtyard: through foreshortening and clever use of light, the colonnade rapidly diminishes in scale, culminating in a statue which is, in fact, tiny.

From Vicolo di Polverone, head across Ponte Sisto and bear right, through Piazza San Giovanni della Malta to Via della Lungara.

> **Palazzo Spada** – Piazza Capo di Ferro 13 (tel: 686-1158). Open: Tuesday to Saturday, 9am–2pm; Sunday, 9am–1pm. Admission charge. For permission to visit the State Rooms, apply to Ufficio Intendenza, Consiglio di Stato, Palazzo Spada, Via Capo di Ferro 3, 00186 Rome.
> **Orto Botanico del Gianicolo** – Open: Monday to Saturday, 9am–7pm (until 6pm October to March), Sunday, 10am–5pm.

4 GALLERIA NAZIONALE D'ARTE ANTICA – PALAZZO CORSINI, see page 52.

Proceed down Via Corsini.

5 ORTO BOTANICO DEL GIANICOLO

Originally the gardens of the Palazzo Corsini, since 1883 this verdant spot has belonged to the University of Rome. Now the Botanical Gardens, they contain some 7,000 plant species.

Proceed back down Via della Lungara and Via della Scala, then turn left for Piazza Santa Maria in Trastevere.

6 SANTA MARIA IN TRASTEVERE, see page 86.

Turn back down Via della Scala and take the first left into Vicolo del Cedro. Turn right into Via Panieri.

7 SANTA MARIA DEI SETTE DOLORI

This church is a minor work by Borromini (1643). Left unfinished, its façade none the less illustrates his fascination with convex and concave surfaces.

Follow Via Garibaldi up to Piazza San Pietro in Montorio.

8 SAN PIETRO IN MONTORIO

The present church was commissioned by Ferdinand and Isabella of Spain in 1481. It contains one of Rome's greatest paintings: Sebastiano del Piombo's *Flagellation of Christ* (1518) for which Michelangelo is said to have prepared the drawings.

Continue along the upper reaches of Via Garibaldi.

9 FONTANA DELL'ACQUA PAOLA

Overlooking Rome from the Gianicolo, this fountain (1610–11) is designed as a triumphal arch. It was a part of Pope Paul V's plan to bring water to Trastevere and the Vatican from the lake of Bracciano, making use of the ancient Acqua Traiana (Trajan's aqueduct).

A short walk to Viale Aldo Fabrizi leads to bus 41. Alight near Ponte Mazzini, cross the river and head east for Campo dei Fiori.

Via Appia Antica

The Via Appia (Appian Way) was ancient Rome's link with its empire in the east. The first section of it, leading out of the old Porta Appia (now the Porta San Sebastiano, see page 71), was built in 312BC, and the road was extended to the ports of Taranto and Brindisi in the 'heel' of Italy in 190BC. Parts of it are still paved and lining its route are the tombs of the Roman patrician dead and the catacombs of the early Christians. *Allow a morning with plenty of time to wait for the bus back into town.*

Take bus 118 from the Colosseum or San Giovanni in Laterano to Porta San Sebastiano. The interesting part of theVia Appia Antica starts beyond the gate.

1 CATACOMBE DI SAN CALLISTO
There are 20km of galleries containing the remains of some 170,000 dead. Carved out of soft volcanic tufa, the burial niches, or *loculli*, are in tiers. The grander dead had separate tombs or entire chapels; tombs of the early popes are generally

---

Catacombe di San Callisto – Via Appia Antica 110 (tel: 513–6725). Open: Thursday to Tuesday, 8.30am–noon and 2.30–5.30pm (until 5pm October to March). Admission charge.
Catacombe di San Sebastiano – Via Appia Antica 136 (tel: 788–7035). Open: Friday to Wednesday, 9am–noon and 2.30–5.30pm (until 5pm October to March). Admission charge.
Tomba di Cecilia Metella – Via Appia Antica, 111 Miglio (tel: 780–2465). Open: Tuesday to Saturday, 9am–sunset (until 2pm October to March), Sunday and Monday, 9am–2pm.

Catacombe di San Callisto ❶

0   100   200   300 m

VICOLO DELLE SETTE CHIESE

APPIA

VIA

Catacombe di San Sebastiano ❷

San Sebastiano

Tomba di Romolo ❸

❹

Circo di Massenzio

PIGNATELLI

ANTICA

Tomba di Cecilia Metella ❺

distinguished by spiralling columns on the side walls of their crypts. Look out, too, for the Crypt of Santa Cecilia (see page 76), the burial place of the saint discovered in AD821.

2 CATACOMBE DI SAN SEBASTIANO

These catacombs were begun in the 1st century BC as a pagan cemetery. St Sebastian was buried here, and the bodies of St Peter and St Paul are supposed to have been brought for safe-keeping. Inscriptions on the wall give credence to these claims. Above the catacombs is the 17th-century church of San Sebastiano, occupying the site of a basilica dating from the reign of Constantine.

3 TOMBA DI ROMOLO

Across the Via Appia is the Tomb of Romolo, son of the tyrant Maxentius, who died in AD309. Not unlike the Pantheon in design, it is placed at the centre of an area enclosed by a four-sided portico. Beyond it lie the ruins of Maxentius' palace.

4 CIRCO DI MASSENZIO

Built in AD309 by Maxentius, this was ancient Rome's last racetrack, 520m long and 92m wide. At its head are the ruins of two towers between which were 12 starting gates for chariot races (see page 160). At the other end was a triumphal arch and down each side were tiers of seats for 10,000 spectators. In the middle of the arena the *spina* was dominated by an obelisk now in the Piazza Navona.

5 TOMBA DI CECILIA METELLA

Built soon after 50BC, this tomb belonged to the wife of Marcus Crassus, son of the rich *triumvir* who ruled Rome

The silent stones of the Appian Way once carried the marching feet of Roman armies

with Pompey and Caesar. In 1302 Pope Boniface gave it to his family and it was turned into a fortress blocking the Via Appia.

Take bus 118 back to the centre.

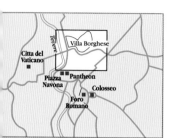

Piazza del Popolo to Via Vittorio Veneto

This walk skirts, then penetrates, the extensive gardens and park of Villa Borghese which contain, in the Casino Borghese (the original 'residence'), the stunning Galleria e Museo Borghese. The park includes a zoo. *Allow a full day and perhaps take a picnic.*

Begin in Piazza del Popolo.

1 PIAZZA DEL POPOLO

Piazza del Popolo evolved over many centuries. It is bounded by the triple-arched Porta del Popolo, the church of Santa

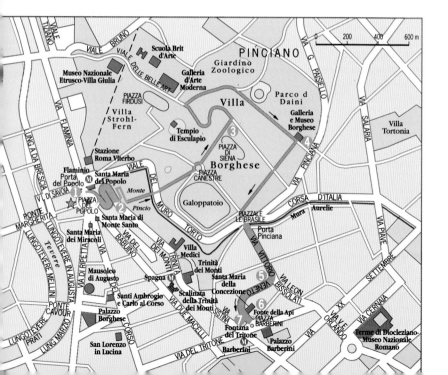

Maria del Popolo (see page 85), the Pincio gardens and the twin churches of Santa Maria in Monte Santo (1672–5, by Bernini, Carlo Fontana and Carlo Rainaldi) and Santa Maria dei Miracoli (Carlo Rainaldi, 1675–9) on opposite sides of Via del Corso. In the square's centre is an obelisk from the Circus Maximus (see page 121), brought to Rome in 10BC. The lions at its base are 19th century.

2 PINCIO

The gardens of the Monte Pincio (Pincian Hill) were laid out in the 19th century and occupy the area of the ancient villas of the Pincii and the Aclii. As well as the obelisk of Antoninus, the collection of busts of distinguished Italians, the café and the benches, the Pincio provides a tremendous view. St Peter's can be seen across the city beyond the domes and façades of Rome's other churches. In the 19th century Pope Pius IX enjoyed his *passeggiata* through the gardens in a carriage drawn by white mules.
From the Pincio proceed east into Villa Borghese.

3 VILLA BORGHESE

On a hot afternoon the extensive, shady gardens of this huge park are a welcome retreat from a noisy city. There is a boating lake, an aviary, fountains, an enormous racetrack (the *Galoppatoio)* as well as the zoo and museum. The park was formerly the estate surrounding Cardinal Scipione Borghese's country retreat, laid out in 1613–16. Altered in the 18th century to resemble English parkland, it was given over to the public in 1902. The park is open daily, 9.00am to dusk.

4 GALLERIA E MUSEO BORGHESE, see page 50.
Exit by Porta Pinciana.

5 VIA VITTORIO VENETO

In the 19th century the beautiful Villa Ludovisi was replaced by houses and apartment blocks. One consolation for the loss has been the undeniable success of Via Vittorio Veneto which cuts through its heart. One of Europe's most fashionable streets, it still has some grand old hotels, pavement cafés and restaurants where, in the 1950s, the *dolce vita* – immortalised by Fellini in his film of that name – played out its course.
Via Vittorio Veneto curves down to Piazza Barberini.

6 FONTANA DELLE API

This Bernini fountain, at the corner of Piazza Barberini and Via Vittorio Veneto, was erected by the Barberini pope Urban VIII in 1644; the bees 'drinking' at the fountain are the armorial symbol of the Barberini family, and the shell-shaped basin is a symbol of life and fertility.

7 FONTANA DEL TRITONE

Bernini's first free-standing fountain (1642–3) is full of allusions to Urban VIII. The merman Triton, perched on scallop shells supported by dolphins, blows on a conch from which a jet of water emerges. He is an emblem of the immortality acquired through literature (Urban was a gifted Latin poet). Dolphins symbolise princely munificence, referring to the pope's patronage of the arts.
To return to Piazza del Popolo, take the Metro in Piazza Barberini and go two stops north to Flaminio.

Monte Aventino

This walk from the Tiber up the steep Aventine Hill includes Roman ruins and two early Christian churches and provides a delectable view over the river. It should be taken at a leisurely pace. *Allow a morning.*

Begin in Piazza Bocca della Verità.

1 TEMPIO DI ERCOLE
Facing the river and long thought to have been dedicated to Vesta, this small circular Temple of Hercules dates from the 2nd century BC. It was converted into a church in the Middle Ages.

2 TEMPIO DI PORTUNUS
Dedicated to the god of rivers and ports, this was another Republican temple converted into a church. On the opposite (east) side of the piazza is the 4th-century Arco di Giano (Arch of Janus).

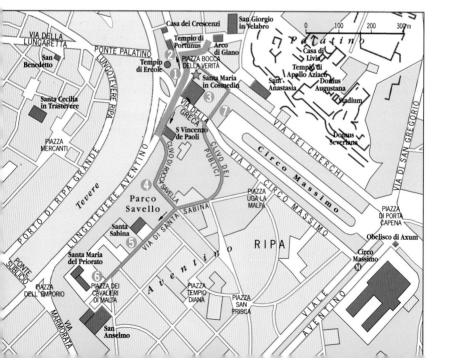

The 7th-century church of San Giorgio in Velabro in the Piazza Bocca della Verità was badly damaged by a bomb in 1993. It took the full force of the blast, protecting Septimius Severus' Arco degli Argentari beside it, and is now closed for restoration.

3 SANTA MARIA IN COSMEDIN

In the porch of this church on the south side of the square is the Bocca della Verità (the Mouth of Truth), a weatherbeaten stone face used as a drain-cover in ancient Rome. According to legend, anyone – but particularly women accused of adultery – putting their right hand into the 'mouth' would have their fingers severed if they lied. See also page 83.

Proceed south, turning left up Clivo di Rocca Savella to Via di Santa Sabina.

4 PARCO SAVELLO

This charming small public garden occupies the site of the old Savelli fortress and provides fine views to the dome of St Peter's.

5 SANTA SABINA

Backing on to Parco Savello, this is one of the most perfectly preserved early Christian basilicas in Rome (see page 80). It was founded in 422 and restored earlier this century, when its 9th-century windows with their selenite windowpanes were uncovered. The mosaic over the entrance is 5th century, while the pulpit, choir and bishop's throne are from the 9th century.

Continue along Via di Santa Sabina.

The interior of Santa Sabina

6 PIAZZA DEI CAVALLIERI DI MALTA

This extraordinary square, with its obelisks and trophies, was designed in 1765 by Giambattista Piranesi, best known as an engraver of views of Roman antiquities and an architectural theorist. The priory gate (number 3) is famous for the bronze keyhole through which can be seen a view of St Peter's in miniature

Go back along Via di Santa Sabina. Descend by way of the Clivo dei Publici.

7 CIRCO MASSIMO

The ancient and much rebuilt Circus Maximus (begun *c.*326BC) could hold 300,000 spectators for the chariot races (see page 160). The stands, on the sides of the Aventine and Palatine hills, lined two long tracks of sand. The imperial box was on the Palatine slope with the general seating below, senators at the top, lesser types on wooden seats below that and *hoi polloi* standing at the bottom. Dividing the track lengthways, but leaving enough room at either end for the chariots to make their turn, was the *spina* on which were an obelisk (now in Piazza del Popolo), statues, seven wooden eggs and seven dolphins. The chariots raced round the *spina,* an egg being removed or the position of a dolphin changed each time a lap was completed.

A short walk in the direction of the river brings you back to Piazza Bocca della Verità.

Excursions

A visit to the countryside around Rome provides a delightful complement to life in the city. To the north, the land is one of high lakes and rivers cut into deep volcanic rock; the country to the south is gentler. Both are regions of hilltowns and castles. All the destinations listed below are within two and a half hours of Rome. Most have places where you can eat, but some require a picnic. For more detailed information and advice on accommodation, local markets and fairs contact local tourist information offices (see TIC telephone numbers after individual entries on pages 124–9), Rome's EPT at Via Parigi 5 (tel: 488–3748) or Lazio's provincial tourist office at Via F Raimondi Garibaldi 7.

Around Rome the hills are dotted with ancient, defensive hilltowns

ROME EXCURSIONS

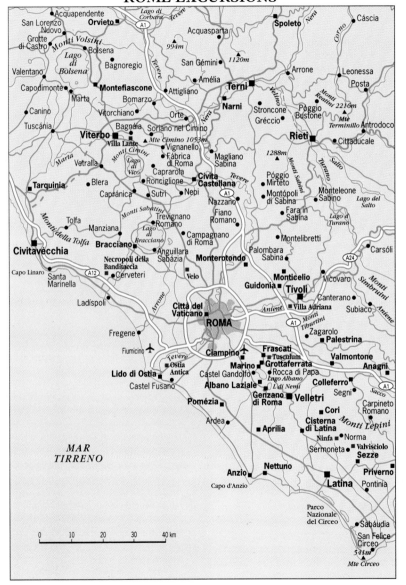

At Bomarzo a stone monster in the Parco dei Mostri tears a woman in half

Romans who like to lunch there.

At **Frascati** (21km from Rome), famous for its white wine, the gardens of the Villas Aldobrandini and Torlonia are open to the public. **Grottaferrata** (27km) is visited for its 11th-century Greek Orthodox abbey and church of Santa Maria. **Marino** (24km) produces some of the region's best wine and **Nemi** (36km) is famous for its strawberries. A dramatic mountain eyrie, **Rocca di Papa** (32km) is dominated by a 12th-century papal fortress, while **Castel Gandolfo** (24km) has the papal summer residence, the Palazzo Papale. The palace and the church of San Tommaso, built by Bernini (frescos by Pietro da Cortona), dominate the main square; choose for lunch a trattoria with views over Lago Albano (Alban Lake), where

BOMARZO

This medieval hilltown clinging to a rocky crag is a warren of tiny alleys and ancient passages. The nearby **Parco dei Mostri** (Monster Park), laid out by the Duke of Orsini in 1552, takes its inspiration from Ariosto's Orlando Furioso. Huge, bizarre stone-carved monsters and crazy summerhouses are scattered about in the 'Sacro' Bosco ('Sacred' Wood). A good spot for children (see page 155). Take a picnic. *TIC: see Viterbo. 95km from Rome. Rail: Termini.*

CASTELLI ROMANI

Thirteen ancient towns in the Colli Albani (Alban Hills) grew up around medieval feudal strongholds or papal fortresses. Many have their own festivals, and are popular at weekends with

THE FARNESE

In the 16th century the Farnese family, of which Pope Paul III was a member, was the most prominent in northern Lazio. The fortress at Capodimonte had belonged to them since 1385 and here lived the beautiful Giulia who, at 16, became the mistress of the Borgia pope Alexander VI. Because of her the Farnese became rich; Alessandro, Giulia's brother, became a cardinal at only 18 and built the Villa Farnese at Caprarola. The family enriched the region with churches, castles, villas, gardens, sculpture and painting, and many places associated with them are open to the public (see Villa Lante page 129).

The necropolis area at Cerveteri. The Etruscan tombs date back to the 6th century BC

there are lidos for swimming. **Albano Laziale** (25km) grew up around Castra Albano, a 2nd-century legionary camp established to defend the Via Appia. *TIC: tel: 932 4081. Rail: Termini, trains to all towns.*

CAPRAROLA

The **Villa Farnese** here, a huge late Renaissance country palace, was built for Cardinal Alessandro Farnese by Vignola and constructed over a pentagonal fortress designed by Sangallo the Younger (1520s). Inside, a vast spiral staircase ascends to a series of chambers decorated by the Zuccaro brothers; the Sala del Mappamondo is splendidly adorned with maps of the world. The palace has lovely gardens, partially private and containing the summer residence of the Italian President. *TIC: see Viterbo. 62km from Rome. Rail: Stazione San Pietro to Viterbo and local buses via Lago di Vico.*

CERVETERI

An important Etruscan city, Cerveteri *(Caere)* has remains of Etruscan and medieval walls and a Romanesque belfry. The Museo Nazionale Cerite houses Etruscan antiquities.

Necropoli della Banditaccia

The Etruscan necropolis lies about 2km from town. Most of what we know about the Etruscans (see box on page 128) comes from excavations of their necropolises, literally 'cities of the dead'. The tombs here, of which the circular *tumuli* with earth-covered domes are the oldest, once contained not only the dead but their possessions for use in the afterlife, and were arranged in streets and squares like houses in a city of the living.

No TIC. Town Hall: tel: 994 2348. 44km from Rome. Rail: Termini. For coach trips: contact CIT (tel: 479 4372) or Carrani (tel: 460 510).

ORVIETO

The medieval hilltown of Orvieto looks much as it did 500 years ago and is a wonderful place to spend a day. The Etruscans founded a settlement here (destroyed by the Romans around 280BC), and there is a 4th-century BC necropolis. In the Middle Ages Orvieto became a stronghold of the Papal States and a retreat for the pope when required.

The magnificent **Duomo** (cathedral), founded in 1290, has a façade rich with mosaics, tracery and sculpture. Begun in the Romanesque style and continued in the Gothic, it is a treasure-house of early Renaissance art with frescos by Gentile da Fabriano, Fra Angelico, Benozzo Gozzoli and Luca Signorelli.

In Piazza del Duomo, the **Museo Civico** contains finds from local Etruscan tombs. Near by, the **Palazzo dei Papi** (Popes' Palace) houses the **Museo del Duomo** with works from the cathedral, including sculptures by Arnolfo di Cambio and the Pisanos, and an altarpiece by Simone Martini.

San Domenico, the first Dominican church ever built (1233), contains a fine tomb sculpted by Arnolfo di Cambio (1281). Under the 12th-century church of **Sant'Andrea** are the ruins of a 6th-century church and beneath this can be seen an Etruscan street and buildings. **San Lorenzo** (14th century) has an Etruscan altar under the Christian high altar and a lovely 12th-century stone canopy above. **Pozzo di San Patrizio** (St Patrick's Well) was dug in the 1530s by order of Clement VII, who fled here following the Sack of Rome, in case Orvieto should come under siege.

TIC: tel: 0763/42562. 102km from Rome. Rail: Termini (90 min).

OSTIA ANTICA

The ancient port of Rome was founded around 338BC to protect the mouth of the Tiber from pirates; its plan resembles that of a castrum (military camp).

Just inside the gate, Porta Romana, the **Terme di Nettuno** (Baths of Neptune), with their heating installations, have fine mosaics. The nearby **theatre**, built in the Augustan age and altered by Septimius Severus, could hold 3,000 spectators. The tiers of seats and the semicircular orchestra have survived. Behind the theatre, the **Piazzale delle Corporazioni** (Corporation Square) was flanked by

Poking up into the heavens, the Duomo, Orvieto

The perfectly preserved theatre at Ostia Antica, where open-air performances are given in summer

commercial offices representing shipping agents from all over the empire. Individual emblems have been preserved: the elephant, for example, is the symbol of the town of Sabrata in North Africa. Near by are the **Casa di Apuleio** (House of Apuleius) with its mosaic pavements, and the **Mitreo delle Sette Sfere** (Mithraeum of the Seven Spheres) with symbol-filled mosaics.

Close to the public and commercial heart of Ostia – the **Capitoleum** and **Forum** the **Tempio di Roma e Augusto** (Temple of Rome and Augusto) has a statue of Rome victorious, dressed as an Amazon. In the Terme di Foro (Forum Baths) are statues of the health divinities Aesculapius and Hygeia and a mosaic of Ostia's ancient lighthouse. To the west is a splendidly preserved large warehouse, the **Horrea Epagathiana**.

At its western extremity the Decumanus Maximus (the main street) diverges: **Via della Foce** leads to three Republican temples – **Hercules Invictus** (unconquered Hercules), **Tempio dell'Ara degli Amorini** (Temple of the Altar of the Cupids) and a third whose dedication is unknown. The **Terme dei Sette Sapienti** (Baths of the Seven Philosophers). are named after the frescos found there featuring Greek philosophers. The final stretch of the Decumanus Maximus runs through an area containing houses (look for the polychrome mosaics in **Domus dei Dioscuri** – House of the Dioscuri), a food market *(macellum)*, shops and the *Caupona dei Pavone*, an inn with a marble floor and walls decorated with figures.

TIC: see Rome. 23km from Rome. Rail: Stazione Ostiense, or Metro from Termini.

A Roman aqueduct still stands at Tarquinia

TARQUINIA

One of the three major centres of
Etruscan civilisation, Tarquinia declined
after the growth of Rome. Many of the
artefacts excavated here are in the
Museo Nazionale Tarquiniese in the
Palazzo Vitelleschi, but visitors generally
head for the cemetery, the **Necropoli di**
Monterozzi. Here the chief attractions
are the wall paintings in the tombs,
mythical and ritualistic scenes or
vignettes from everyday life, put there to
remind the dead of life. There are some
6,000 tombs, including 62 fully or partly
painted: the **Tomba dei Leopardi** and
Tomba degli Auguri have particularly
evocative paintings.
*TIC: 0766/ 856 384. 88km from Rome.
Rail: Termini.*

THE ETRUSCANS

Sophisticated, powerful, prosperous,
the Etruscan civilisation flourished
and was paramount in central Italy
from the 8th to 4th century BC.
Shrewd merchants, the Etruscans
traded all round the Mediterranean
with the result that their culture
assimilated ideas and innovations
from more advanced civilisations in
the region. Yet Etruria was not so
much a nation as a federation of
autonomous cities, such as Tarquinia
and Cerveteri. Etruscan civilisation
declined under first Greek then
Roman expansion in Italy and
ultimately became absorbed into that
of Rome.

TIVOLI

Tivoli has long been celebrated for its
healthy air and lovely landscapes, and the
ruins of **Villa Adriana**, Hadrian's
summer palace, are here. The emperor
conceived his palace as a compendium of
the most beautiful architecture he had
seen during his travels, and enough
remains to evoke its vast and luxurious
scale. **Villa d'Este**, built in 1550 by
Cardinal Ippolito d'Este, son of Lucrezia
Borgia, has magnificent gardens filled
with fountains and formal terraces. With
their profusion of jets and sprays and
quirky designs, the fountains display
great inventiveness. The **Villa**

Gregoriana is a park with waterfalls created in 1831, when Pope Gregory XVI redirected the River Aniene to prevent it flooding Tivoli.
TIC: 0774/ 21 249. 31km from Rome. Rail: Termini.

TUSCÁNIA
The chief reason to visit this little walled town, severely damaged in an earthquake (1971), is to see the lovely Romanesque basilicas of **Santa Maria Maggiore** and **San Pietro**, the latter one of the best of its date in Italy. Standing some way out of town, both are 8th century though rebuilt in the 11th, 12th, and 13th centuries, when the rest of Tuscania was built up and walled.
TIC: see Viterbo. 71km from Rome, 24km from Viterbo.

VITERBO
Viterbo rivalled Rome in importance in the Middle Ages, when it was the official seat of several popes. The 13th-century **Palazzo del Podestà**, adjacent to the **Palazzo dei Priori** (1460), is at its civic heart. **Palazzo Papale** (13th century) with a beautiful arcaded loggia was the Papal Palace, and the nearby Romanesque **Cattedrale** occupies the site of the ancient Etruscan acropolis. The **Quartiere di San Pellegrino**, a labyrinthine medieval quarter, contains 11th-century **Santa Maria Nuova** and its cloister, a magnificent example of Romanesque architecture. The church of **Santa Rosa** contains the blackened corpse of St Rosa, Viterbo's 13th-century patron saint. The **Museo Civico** contains various Etruscan and Roman artefacts as well as Sebastiano del

Piombo's magnificent Pietà, for which Michelangelo provided the drawings.

Villa Lante
Four kilometres from Viterbo, the beautiful gardens of the Villa Lante are among the greatest surviving examples of late Renaissance horticulture. They were laid out in the 16th century by Giacomo Barozzi da Vignola, for the Farnese Cardinal Gambara, on five terraces incorporating fountains, cascades and waterfalls. With water-powered automata and water tricks hidden inside carved stone fountains the gardens' function was to amuse and entertain.
TIC: 0761/346363. 110km from Rome. Rail: Stazione San Pietro on Roma-Nord line (2hrs).

Artful displays: one of the many fountains in the formal terraced gardens at the Villa d'Este

THE GRAND TOUR

Throughout the 18th century, travel and study on the European continent were considered essential training for young gentlemen of fortune from the British Isles, an ideal means of gaining taste, knowledge, self-assurance and polished manners. It was an invaluable alternative or supplement to a university education. A five-year sojourn abroad was not unknown: young men would travel through France to Italy, staying in Venice, Florence and Rome, returning via Switzerland, Germany, Austria and the Netherlands.

Rome, full of magnificent churches, palaces and 'ancient and modern curiosities' was 'the great crown of their travels', said one traveller. Some, like James Boswell and Robert Adam, studied antiquities, pictures, architecture and the other arts in detail, armed with maps, plans, magnifying glasses, sketch-pads and guidebooks, and conscientiously recording their impressions. Others, less earnest, hurriedly inspected highlights like the Sistine Chapel and Vatican Library, the Baths of Diocletian and Santa Maria Maggiore before making for the fleshpots or – for gruesome entertainment – the places of public execution. Richer grand tourists, like the Earls of Burlington, Leicester and Carlisle, came back with souvenirs: collections of statuary and paintings, or portraits of themselves posing against a backdrop of some notable antiquity.

In Britain the consequences of the Grand Tour were enormous. Travellers returned from Mediterranean lands with a knowledge of and taste for the Greek and Roman past, so that neo-classical

Byron, visiting Italy as a grand tourist, contemplates the ruins of Rome

design, particularly in architecture, became prevalent in the 18th century. Country houses were turned into 'classical' palaces while their parks were adorned with pavilions and temples to evoke the ancient past. This period was a highlight of English architecture, and Rome was its inspiration.

GETTING AWAY FROM IT ALL

The vines, climbing to the
summit of the trees, reach in
festoons and fruitages from
one tree to another, planted
at exact distances, forming a
more delightful picture than
painting can describe.

JOHN EVELYN

A golden oriole feeding her family

ISOLE PONTINE

Off the coast at Monte Circeo on the edge of the Gulf of Gaeta are the Pontine Islands – Ponza, Zannone, Palmarola, Santo Stefano and Ventotene. These are Italy's least visited coastal islands, perhaps better described as rocks with a smattering of vegetation. Take a weekend away from Rome to visit them.

Ponza

Ponza is the biggest – only 1,500m

CIRCE'S ISLAND

Monte Circeo was identified by some classical writers as Aeaea, the island of Circe, daughter of Helios the sun-god. She was a powerful witch, and around her house prowled lions and wolves, the transformed human victims of her sorcery. Far from being dangerous, they fawned on anyone who approached. Odysseus stopped here on his voyage home from the Trojan war, and lived with Circe for a year, protected from her treachery by a drug given him by the god Hermes.

---

across at its widest – with a dramatically varied coastline of inlets and bays, tiny secluded beaches and strange volcanic rock formations. Its main town, also called Ponza, is a huddle of pink- and white-washed houses straddling the port. La Forna is an attractive seaside hamlet filled with bleached-white, square cottages and chapels. Ponza is the best base in the islands as it has a variety of places to stay and eat.

Zannone, part of the Circeo National Park, can be visited from Ponza, as can **Palmarola** which, although uninhabited now, has the remains of a cave-dwelling community whose homes were dug out of the cliffsides.

Ventotene

Ventotene can also be reached from Ponza. Its main settlement occupies the site of the former Roman port, once a punitive colony. Banished to its remote shores were Julia, daughter of Augustus, Agrippina, wife of Germanicus, and Octavia, the barren wife of Nero. Flatter and less green than Ponza, Ventotene is truly remote, and supports a population of only 500. There are a few tiny hotels, and guests can also stay in private homes.

Getting there

Ponza: ferry or hydrofoil from Formia (1 hour 15 minutes), ferry from Terracina (1 hour) and hydrofoil from Anzio (1 hour 10 minutes). Hydrofoils are more expensive than ferries, but take under half as long.

Ventotene: ferry or hydrofoil from Formia or Anzio (3 hours by ferry).

Ponza to Ventotene by hydrofoil (40 minutes).

Above: bee-eaters   Below: white stork

PARCO NAZIONALE DEL CIRCEO

In 1934 the Circeo National Park was established on a flat, watery stretch of coastline in the shadow of Monte Circeo to preserve a naturally marshy environment long rendered uninhabitable by malaria, but deemed to be of special interest for its flora and fauna. Originally part of the Pontine Marshes, which were drained in 1928, this is one of Italy's smallest parks and it includes the wooded Monte Circeo as well as the Pontine island of Zannone, a haven for migratory birds. The park surrounds Sabaudia, an interesting monument to Fascist town-planning, and includes the little town of San Felice Circeo and four coastal lakes.

Circeo National Park is a bird-watcher's paradise. Apart from the herons, storks, buzzards, fishhawks and peregrine falcons, numerous other birds, including the golden oriole, the little egret and the spotted woodpecker, have been seen. Wild boar and roe deer also roam among the ash, elm and eucalyptus groves. This is a splendid place to walk in, and the nearby waters of Terracina's beaches are clean enough for swimming.

Getting there

By car: SS148 (65km)

By train: Termini to Terracina, and then a local bus to Sabaudia.

By bus: Rome (Via Gaeta) to Latina, and then a local bus.

To the north of Sabaudia, at Via Carlo Alberto 2, is the park information centre (tel: 0773 511387).

Peaceful respite from city life at the Lago di Vico nature reserve

RISERVA NATURALE
LAGO DI VICO

Lake Vico is northern Lazio's smallest and highest lake, lying deeper in its crater bed than the lakes of Bolsena or

---

HERCULEAN ORIGINS

Hercules is supposed to have visited this area. Indeed it is due to him, according to local legend, that Lake Vico exists. Asked by some shepherds to demonstrate his strength, Hercules stuck his club into the ground and invited them to try to pull it out. One by one they failed, and even when they pulled together the club stayed firm. Eventually Hercules pulled it out himself and, from the hole, gushed water. At the same time the mountains rose forming a crater which became Lake Vico.

Bracciano on either side of it. To the west are the forests of Monte Cimini and to the north the Valle di Vico, a marshy wetland home to many varieties of birds, flowers and strange grasses. The highest point above the lake, also to the north, is the conical Monte Venere, once an almost circular island. All this is protected now by the Lake Vico Nature Reserve. The lake's waters are clean and delightful to swim in, and there are good walks to be had around its shore. Way above the lake the Via Ciminia cuts across the summits overlooking the water. Apart from the views up here, there is a whole host of little restaurants where you can have lunch. See Caprarola, page 125.

Getting there

By car: the SS2 road to Viterbo passes to the west of the lake.

By train: in Rome, Stazione San Pietro

links with Viterbo from which there are local buses to Lago di Vico.

VILLA CELIMONTANA

On the Celian Hill (see page 29), the Villa Celimontana is the biggest and greenest open space in an area dotted with archaeological remains, medieval monastery buildings and churches. Just on the edge of central Rome, not far from the Colosseum and adjacent to the Palatine Hill, it is accessible, quiet and beautiful, a perfect spot for a picnic between bouts of sightseeing. In the heat of the day, you can sit in the shade and read or feed the cats.

The park surrounds a 16th-century summerhouse, once the property of the Mattei family and now the headquarters of the Italian Geographical Society. The best way in is from the piazza in front of Santi Giovanni e Paolo (see page 113); from a large wrought-iron gate a path leads to the heart of the park through avenues of trees, past palms and the occasional obelisk. The gardens once

Above: the quiet life at Villa Celimontana
Below, left: away from the bustle of the streets

contained important Egyptian sculptures, but were transformed into the informal 'English' style in the 19th century.

To leave the park, take a different route to come out in Piazza della Navicella beside the church of Santa Maria in Domnica, famed for its 9th-century mosaics. Then return to the city centre through the Arco di Dolabella (built AD10 and later used to carry a section of Nero's Acqua Claudia extension delivering water to the imperial palace on the Palatine) and along the narrow Via San Paolo della Croce leading past Santi Giovanni e Paolo. *Piazza della Navicella. Park open: daily, 7am to dusk. Bus: 15, 81, 85, 87, 90, 118.*

The park of the Villa Doria Pamphili

VILLA DORIA PAMPHILI

The Princes and Princesses Doria Pamphili used to escape the noise and bustle of metropolitan life by retiring to their villa behind Trastevere on the slope of the Gianicolo (Janiculum Hill). Nowadays the grounds belong to the state and everybody else does the same. However, unless you come by taxi, the park is not really convenient for a quick picnic in the middle of sightseeing. It is more of an 'afternoon-off' kind of park, somewhere to go for a long, lazy walk, to sit and read a book or to jog.

The partially wild park is huge. Its boundary wall carries the Acqua Paola aqueduct and its centrepiece is a magnificent building called the Casino del Bel Respiro, probably designed by Alessandro Algardi for the Pamphili pope Innocent X (1644–55). The casino was meant purely for entertaining and has no bedrooms. Outside, the walls are adorned with displays of ancient sculpture, and the gardens all around were laid out in the 17th century for Prince Camillo Pamphili, although they were altered in the 19th century. They still contain a number of grottoes and fountains, terraces and walks. The most interesting feature is Bernini's Fountain of the Snail: it is thought that he designed it for the Piazza Navona but that Innocent X rejected it as too small and insignificant for such a site. The Pope's imperious sister-in-law, Donna Olimpia, is said to have claimed the fountain for the villa's garden. What you see now is a replacement, the original having found its way into the Palazzo Doria Pamphili where it remains.
Via di San Pancrazio. Park open: daily, dawn to dusk. Bus: 41, 75, 144.

DIRECTORY

Rome is a continuity, called
'eternal'. What has
accumulated in this place acts
on everyone day and night,
like an extra climate.

ELIZABETH BOWEN,
A Time in Rome (1960)

Shopping

*R*ome is much like any other major Italian city when it comes to searching for a representative selection of the 'best' of what the country has to offer. But as a capital city, it lacks the choice and variety of, say, Paris or London. Indeed, if you are looking for clothing you might do better in Florence or Milan unless you want couture or hand-made accessories worked with beads or some other intricate finish.

Nevertheless, shopping in Rome is far from disappointing. The city is well stocked with things to buy: designer clothes, shoes and accessories, state-of-the-art lighting equipment and kitchenware, fabrics and textiles, rustic-style ceramics, fine art, antique furniture, food and wine. Many artisan traditions are kept alive and old workshops are scattered through the city, making jewellery, gilding gesso picture frames,

Looking for inexpensive imitations, Via del Corso

cabinet-making, restoring marbles – and only too ready to welcome you in to show you how it's done.

One of the best things about shopping in Rome is that you can shop late, often up to 8.30pm. If you intend having a picnic supper, this allows you to buy the ingredients fresh. It also means you can return to a shop where you saw an interesting item earlier in the day, try it on at leisure, then take it straight to your hotel. After all, who wants to carry a new pair of shoes around all day? The late

VALENTINO

Rome is the home of Valentino, Italy's golden boy of *haute couture* and its most successful commercial fashion designer. His name (he was born Valentino Garavani) must be as well known as that of Fiat's Agnelli. Since he opened his first business in Via Condotti in 1959, later expanding into Via Gregoriana, he has dressed many of the world's richest and most famous women. He has maintained a loyal following for his glamorous and elegant clothes, which he bases on the 1950s Hollywood look. The 1980s marked the apogee of his fame and fortune, and he has since moved into a huge *palazzo* in Piazza Mignanelli, near the Spanish Steps. Note the 'V' above the entrance portal.

shopping hours do have certain disadvantages: assistants are sometimes tired and irritable and shops tend to be very crowded.

Best Buys

What might you buy that typifies the 'best' of Italian merchandise? For the kitchen, aluminium or stainless steel coffee-makers, kettles and everyday cooking implements made by Alessi are good buys, as are the huge spongeware saladbowls and pots imported from Abruzzo and Apulia. Bottles of thick, green virgin olive oil or oil impregnated with *peperoncini* are generally cheaper in Italy than they are abroad. So too are packets of *funghi porcini* (dried mushrooms), bunches of herbs and spices from Campo dei Fiori market, salamis, local *pecorino* cheese, parmesan

A restoration workshop

Evening entertainment

and olives. Buy food at the last minute.

Italy is obviously the best place to buy clothes with Italian 'designer' labels; most are represented in Rome. But look out for well-made, inexpensive imitations: with careful choice, many a wardrobe can be elegantly kitted out with fakes. Some very good second-hand shops sell leather jackets and coats, and suede jackets and trousers, and there are ex-army and navy coats, fatigues, boots, and such like, to be had in the markets. Rome, with its artisan goldsmith and silversmith tradition, is a good place to buy contemporary jewellery, while cheap souvenirs might come from the 'pilgrim' shops near the big churches, or from the stalls near the Forum. And of course there are endless T-shirts to be had with an interesting array of designs evoking memories of the Eternal City.

SHOPPING AREAS

Rome's shops are often grouped together in a single street or neighbourhood according to merchandise or artisan tradition. Sometimes this convention has its roots in the distant past, when a street might have been named after the traditional craft of its residents, and there are enclaves all over the city where the practice has survived. This makes it easier to compare prices and styles, quite apart from the fact that it adds significantly to the neighbourhood's character.

Via Condotti

This is where you will find the most chic and expensive clothes, shoes and accessories (not necessarily Italian). Both men's and women's fashion are well represented. Max Mara, Salvatore Ferragamo, Gucci, Louis Vuitton, Hermes, Bulgari, Van Cleef and Arpels, Valentino and Prada jostle for space, each shop-window an exercise in

> ### FARMACIA SANTA MARIA DELLA SCALA
> One of the oldest dispensaries in Europe to have survived intact and still in operation, this 18th-century pharmacy within the 16th-century Carmelite monastery once supplied herbal cures and potions to the popes and their families. Today you can buy digestive liquors in its frescoed interior.
> *Piazza Santa Maria della Scala. Open: daily, 9am–11am. Donation expected*

haughty one-upmanship. These are the kind of shops where the staff can be so intimidating that browsers tend to prefer window-shopping. *Passeggiata* – the dusk stroll so beloved of Italians – engulfs Via Condotti every evening as it moves on towards the Spanish Steps.

Serious shopping at the best and the most expensive end of the market

Via Frattina, Via Borgognona, Via Bocca di Leone and Piazza di Spagna

These streets contain Via Condotti's overspill. Apart from one or two shops (most notably Gianni Versace) the windows here are slightly less flamboyant. This is a good area for shoes, handbags, gloves, belts and other accessories.

Via della Croce

This street specialises in good food. Among the bars and cafés with their heaps of delicious filled sandwiches and *panini* (rolls) are some of Rome's best delicatessens, where you can buy virtually anything from *zucchini* flowers to olive oil impregnated with the flavour of wild mushrooms.

Other concentrations of food shops are found around Santa Maria della Pace (behind Piazza Navona), in Campo dei Fiori (see page 144) and in the Ghetto (see page 53).

Via del Babuino

In spite of its inelegant name *(babuino* means baboon), this is one of Rome's most elegant and expensive streets. It is lined with shops selling everything from old masters, modern art (see also Via Margutta, just to the east), quality antique furniture, silver, old porphyry vases and dishes and marble statues to up-to-date kitchen equipment, modern glassware and lighting fixtures.

Via del Corso

This long street is the poor relation to Via Condotti, being the purveyor of cheaper copies of the exclusive items on sale in the latter. Many scorn it but, along with Via del Tritone and Via Nazionale, it is the source of inexpensive

Passeggiata in the Via Condotti

Italian shoes, jackets, jeans, scarves, Ralph Lauren rip-offs, Versace lookalikes and Chanel wannabees.

Via dei Coronari, Via dell'Orso, Via dei Soldati

Even if you are not looking for antique tables and gilded mirrors, Murano chandeliers and battered pictures of the saints, these three neighbouring streets still make an interesting evening stroll. There are cabinet-makers, marble restorers, interesting old doorways and courtyards and the omnipresent café in which to refresh yourself. More antique shops are to be found in exclusive Via Giulia (see page 107), Via Fontanella Borghese and Via Sistina, while Via del Governo Vecchio is the source of antique and second-hand clothes at extremely reasonable prices. Ancient Via dei Cappellari (the 'street of the hatmakers'), Via Monserrato and Via del Pellegrino are where the cabinet-makers are grouped.

Tabacchi shop

The following is a representative list of shops providing particular items that a visitor to Rome might consider buying. Specialist clothes shops are not included; the main streets in which to find them have already been mentioned (see pages 140-1).

ANTIQUES
Amadeo di Castro
Mostly 18th- and 19th-century pieces.
Via del Babuino 77/78 (tel: 320 7650).
Antiquario Valligiano
19th-century country furniture.
Via Giulia 193 (tel: 686 9505).
Granmercato Antiquario Babuino
The nearest thing Rome has to an antiques market. Silver, porcelain, etc.
Via del Babuino 150 (tel: 323 5686).
Piero Talone
Just one shop in a street of over 40 specialising in mostly baroque and Empire pieces.
Via dei Coronari 135 (tel: 687 5450).

ARTE SACRA
The best of the shops selling such items as priestly vestments, candles, etc are to be found in and around Via dei Cestari. There are others in the Via della Conciliazione.

BOOKS AND STATIONERY
Cartoleria Artistica
Postcards (old and new) of practically every feature of interest in Rome.
Piazza della Rotonda 69a (tel: 679 0483).
Feltrinelli
Contemporary literature.
Via del Babuino 39/41 (tel: 323 5519).
Franco Mario Ricci
Outlet for beautiful art books and its own 'art' magazine FMR.
Via Borgognona 4D (tel: 679 3466).
Laboratorio Scatole
Writing paper, pretty containers.
Via della Steletta 27 (tel: 68 80 2053).
Libreria San Silvestro
Reduced price art books.
Piazza San Silvestro 27 (tel: 679 2824).
Lion Bookshop
Specialist in English books.
Via del Babuino (tel: 322 5837).
Pineider
Upmarket stationery, visiting cards and desk equipment.
Via dei Due Macelli 68 (tel: 678 9013).
Rizzoli
Italy's largest bookshop. Cookery, architecture, guidebooks and novels; also books in English.
Largo Chigi 15 (tel: 679 6641).
Vertecchi
Via della Croce 70 (tel: 678 3110) and Via dei Gracchi 179 (tel: 321 3559).

DEPARTMENT STORES
Coin
Cheap clothes and good Italian kitchenware.

Piazzale Appio (tel: 708 0020).

Standa

Cheap clothes.

Via Cola di Rienzo (tel: 324 3283).

UPIM

Cheap clothes and household goods.

Piazza Santa Maria Maggiore (tel: 446 5579), Via del Tritone (tel: 678 3336).

FABRICS

Bises

Excellent linens, fashion fabrics and silks.

205 C Francia (tel: 678 9156).

Cesari

Excellent linens and silks for upholstery.

Via del Babuino 16 (tel: 361 1441).

FOOD AND WINE

Castroni

Coffee, olive oils, balsamic vinegar.

Via Cola di Rienzo 196 (tel: 687 4383).

Cisternino Cooperativo fra Produttori di Latte di Lazio

Good for local cow's, sheep's and buffalo's milk cheeses.

Vicolo del Gallo 20 (tel: 687 2875).

Enoteca Buccone

An excellent wine shop.

Via di Ripetta 19 (tel: 361 2154).

Fior Fiore

Lavish delicatessen and grocery store.

Via della Croce 17/18 (tel: 679 1386).

Fratelli Fabbi

Excellent grocery store.

Via della Croce 27 (tel: 679 0612).

Pietro Franchi

Lavish delicatessen with a fine array of take-away food and grocery items.

Via Cola di Rienzo 204 (tel: 683 2669).

Roffi Isabelli

Large selection of local wines and olive oils. Wine can be tasted here in a quaint old setting.

Via della Croce 76B (tel: 679 0896).

JEWELLERY

Boncompagni Sturni

Good quality traditional gold and silver jewellery.

Via del Babuino 115 (tel: 678 3847).

Bulgari

Huge jewels at huge prices.

Via Condotti 10 (tel: 679 3876).

Massoni

Established in the 18th century, they sell classic designs and one-offs.

Largo Carlo Goldoni 48 (tel: 678 2679).

Oddi e Seghetti

Traditional artisan-style designs. They also work to commission.

Via del Cancello 18 (tel: 68 80 2643).

Petochi

Former Italian royal jeweller; both traditional and contemporary pieces. Very expensive.

Piazza di Spagna 23 (tel: 679 3947).

KITCHENWARE

Croff (Centro Casa)

Inexpensive kitchenware, crockery, glass, linen and furniture.

Via Tomacelli 137 (tel: 687 8385).

CUCINA

Upmarket, chic kitchenware.

Via del Babuino 118A (tel: 684 0819).

Picture paradise on Via Margutta

MARKETS

CAMPO DEI FIORI

This large and colourful fruit and vegetable market is flanked by delicatessens and is a good place to buy a picnic. A solitary old cart selling junk is the last reminder of the flea market on this spot that was moved to the Porta Portese area after World War II. Executions once took place here, a history quite at odds with the square's charming name, which means 'Field of Flowers'.

Monday to Saturday, 7am–2pm. Buses: 46, 62, 64, 90 90b.

MERCATO ANDREA DORIA

This market's location away from the centre has kept the tourists at bay and the prices down, making it a good venue for the bargain-hungry shopper

The outdoor life of
Rome's markets is colourful
and ebullient

in search of fruit and vegetables, meat
and fish, clothes and shoes.
*Via Andrea Doria: Monday to Saturday,
7am–1pm. Buses: 23, 70. Metro:
Ottaviano.*

MERCATO DI PIAZZA VITTORIO EMANUELE II

Anything, and everything, from live
chickens to shoelaces, can be found
here. Kitchen equipment, clothes,
shoes, leather goods and cassettes are
some of the good buys on offer.
*Piazza Vittorio Emanuele II: Monday to
Saturday, 7am–2pm. Buses: 4, 9, 11,
70, 71. Metro: Vittorio Emanuele.*

MERCATO DELLE STAMPE

This tiny market sells second-hand art
books, prints, postcards and maps.
*Largo della Fontanella di Borghese:
Monday to Saturday, 7am–1pm. Buses:
23, 70. Metro: Ottaviano.*

PORTA PORTESE

Rome's vast flea market has two arms
fanning out from the Portese Gate on
the edge of Trastevere. To the left find
cheap new clothing, shoes, cassettes,
luggage, jewellery, kitchenware,
sunglasses and ex-army equipment. To
the right are junk stalls with old
furniture and church candlesticks,
pictures, china, statues, pots and pans.
Avoid the parallel arm, particularly after
11.00am when it gets very crowded.
*Via Portuense and Via Ippolito Nievo:
Sundays only, 6.30am–2pm. Buses:
170, 280, 718, 719.*

VIA SANNIO

Long heralded as Rome's answer to
London's Carnaby Street, this is the
haunt of bargain-hunting pensioners
and students. Come here for second-
hand fur coats, suede jackets, ex-army
equipment, Levis and cheap new shoes.
*Via Sannio: Monday to Saturday,
8am–1pm. Buses: 16, 81, 87. Metro:
San Giovanni.*

Entertainment

Come to Rome in summer to enjoy the best of the city's cultural events, particularly classical music and opera. To find out what's on, consult the daily newspapers and the special listings sheets (see box below).

BALLET AND DANCE

The **Teatro dell'Opera** (see box on page 147) has a resident ballet company, the Corpo di Ballo del Teatro dell'Opera, which performs either at its own venue or, in the summer, in the **Terme di Caracalla** (but check that it has not been cancelled – see page 148). Modern dance is often performed at the **Teatro Olimpico**. Check the listings for guest dance companies in Rome for summer festivals.

Teatro Olimpico, *Piazza Gentile da Fabriano 17 (tel: 323 4908 or 323 4936)*.
Terme di Caracalla, *Viale di Terme di Caracalla 52 (tel: 575 8302). Metro: Colosseo.*

CINEMA

Foreign films tend to be dubbed into Italian rather than subtitled. A single cinema, Pasquino, regularly shows commercial films in English. Alcazar, one of the few cinemas which take telephone bookings, is very up-to-date and comfortable (a so-called 'prima visione' cinema) showing English films on Mondays, and sometimes for a whole week. You might also find original language films at what are called 'cinemas d'essai' ('art cinemas'); Labirinto is one of these, a cine-club where you need membership (for a very small fee) to attend.

Pasquino, *Vicolo del Piede 19, Trastevere (tel: 580 3622)*.
Alcazar, *Via Cardinal Merry del Val 14 (tel: 588 0099)*.
Labirinto, *Via di Pompeo Magno 27 (tel: 321 6283)*.

GETTING TICKETS

Booking tickets in advance can be difficult in Rome, as many theatres do not sell seats to telephone callers. However, advance booking is not essential for all events, opera being the big exception. Opera tickets are often sold months in advance, but a few are

---

LISTINGS

Carnet:: monthly, from EPT office.
Here's Rome: English monthly.
Metropolitan: English fortnightly. From newsstands (try the one next to Largo Torre Argentina 11) and the English Bookshop.
Musei e Monumenti di Roma: details of current changes and closures as well as information about exhibitions. From EPT office (see Tourist Information, page 189).
Trovaroma: very comprehensive 'what's on' guide. Published Thursdays with *La Repubblica*; available from newsstands.
Un Anno a Roma e Provincia: details of annual festivals, pageants and fairs. From EPT office.
For daily information about cinema, theatre and cultural events see Rome's newspaper *Il Messaggero*, or city editions of the national papers *La Repubblica* and *Corriere della Sera*.

Opera: indoors in winter, outdoors in summer

generally kept back until the event, so you might be able to snap up something at the last moment.

Central ticket agencies will charge a fee to make a booking for you, usually about 10 per cent of the ticket price. Try **Box Office** for classical music, big jazz, pop and rock events and theatre; **Gesman** for theatre tickets; and **Botteghino,** who will deliver theatre and concert tickets to your hotel reception. **Orbis** supplies tickets for major jazz, pop and rock events, as does **Prontospettacolo,** which takes telephone bookings. Opera tickets can be bought from the box office of the Teatro dell'Opera (box office hours: 10am–1pm and 5–7pm..

A society watering hall

BOOKING AGENCIES
Box Office, Via Giulio Cesare 88 (tel: 372 0215).
Gesman, Via Angelo Emo 65 (tel: 631 803).
Botteghino (tel: 678 3750).
Orbis, Piazza dell'Esquilino 37 (tel: 474 4776 or 482 27403).
Prontospettacolo, 220 Via Aurelia (tel: 39 38 7297).
Teatro dell'Opera, Piazza Beniamino Gigli 8 (tel: 481 7003; in English, tel: 67 59 5725).

Music

Classical Music

Of all the cultural diversions in Rome, classical music offers the most numerous and most varied venues: concert halls, churches, gardens, villas, ruins and ancient palaces. And there is an equal variety of music to be heard. Look out for posters outside churches and leaflets on the tables just inside to find out what concerts are forthcoming. Some churches – San Paolo Fuori le Mura, San Giovanni in Laterano and Sant'Ignazio, for example – have choral masses on certain days of the year. In others you can hear Gregorian chants. Open-air concerts are often held in the **Villa Giulia** gardens (see page 58) and in the **Terme di Caracalla** (but see under **Opera** below). In July wonderful concerts are held in Bramante's cloisters adjacent to Santa Maria della Pace, while the Villa Doria-Pamphili (see page 136) has open-air night-time concerts. Keep an eye on the summer listings for other open-air events.

Rome has three main auditoriums each with its own resident orchestra or choir: **Accademia di Santa Cecilia** (the company, Rome's best, moves to Villa Giulia in the summer – see above), **Auditorium del Foro Italico** and the **Teatro dell'Opera**. Each has its own national and international series with ticket prices up to L20,000 for all but the Teatro dell'Opera, where they can cost over L100,000. The **Teatro Olimpico** (for details see **Ballet and Dance**, page 146) has excellent chamber music, and also sometimes hosts the Accademia Filarmonica. Try the **Oratorio del Gonfalone** for baroque music and choral recitals. Again check the listings for other details and venues.

Accademia di Santa Cecilia, *Via della Conciliazione 4 (tel: 688 01044 or 686 4759).*

Auditorium del Foro Italico, *Piazza Lauro de Bosis 5 (tel: 36 86 5625).*

Oratorio del Gonfalone, *Via del Gonfalone 32A (tel: 687 5952).*

Opera

Opera is performed at the Teatro dell'Opera during the season November to June, and in the open air at the Terme di Caracalla from June to September (for booking and ticket details see box on page 147). Note, however, that the open-air opera season may be cancelled as there is considerable local opposition: it is feared that the high level of sound and the many visitors may be damaging the structure of the baths. A new outdoor location may be provided. If they go ahead, performances last from 9pm to 1am, but nobody will mind if you turn up late, so informal is the occasion.

Rock and Pop

Rome is on the itinerary of some of the biggest names in the modern music business: Madonna, Michael Jackson, Duran-Duran, Peter Gabriel and Prince. Rock and pop concerts are held primarily in the **Palazzo dello Sport** in EUR, but there are a number of other venues such as the **Stadio Olimpico** and the **Stadio Flaminio**. The Orbis agency (see box on page 147) is the place to get tickets (open: Monday to Friday, 9.30am–1pm and 4–7.30pm; Saturday, 10am–1pm). Look in the

The ubiquitous billboards proclaim what's on in the city

popular music magazine, Rockerilla, for details, or call Orbis for information. Be sure to watch the rock channels on television. There is a free 24-hour Video Music channel showing concerts, interviews, and such like.

Palazzo dello Sport, *Viale dell'Umanesimo (tel: 592 5107).*
Stadio Flaminio, *Viale Pilsudski (tel: 323 6539).*
Stadio Olimpico, *Viale dei Gladiatori (tel: 36 85 7520).*

Late night venue

NIGHTCLUBS AND DISCOTHEQUES

There are nightclubs in Rome to suit all tastes. Keep an eye on the listings papers, particularly *Trovaroma*, to see what is new and what has changed – though many of Rome's clubs have stayed the same for years and only occasionally do you find the 'one-nighters' so popular in London. The general idea seems to be to dress up as much as possible, then stand around looking bored. Perhaps the funkiest are the gay clubs, in particular **L'Alibi**, for men and women; try also the centrally located **Hangar** (go late). The music is better at gay clubs than in the straight ones. Thursday and Friday are good clubbing nights, but on Saturday the clubs tend to get very crowded. An alternative would be to hang out around the deeply trendy **Bar della Pace**, adjacent to the little church of Santa Maria della Pace (see page 111) where Rome's moodiest, drop-dead chic younger generation congregate to sit at the little tables where, oddly, they drink nothing at all.

FESTIVAL DEI DUE MONDI
(Festival of the Two Worlds)

Held at Spoleto in Umbria, a drive of some 117km from Rome, this international festival of music, opera, ballet, cinema and art runs for 20 days from 29 June to 18 July. It is one of the great attractions of central Italy and, if you intend to be in Rome for some time during the summer, a visit to the Festival is well worth the effort. Not only is Spoleto a lovely hilltown filled with medieval and Renaissance architecture, but the superb programme put on by composer Giancarlo Menotti, the festival's founder, is generally thought worth trekking halfway across the world for. Top companies and world-class performers are always in attendance. Said Menotti in 1993: 'In these dark times for Italy, overwhelmed by moral, economic and political questions, the Festival is in good shape ... none of us has been imprisoned.' For further information, tickets and programme of events refer to the EPT in Rome (see page 189), or apply direct to the local tourist office in Spoleto (Piazza Libertà) or the Festival's own box office (Piazza del Duomo, tel: 0743/49890).

At the gilded end of the scale, try **Jackie O** for a lavish *haute-bourgeoisie* night out. **Caffè Latino** is good for jazz, **La Makumba** is a late, hot club for *aficionados* of Brazilian and African music, and **RadioLondra** is a free, busy and very loud club filled with gays, straights ... in fact everybody. There are plenty of other places providing the full works from salsa through Hi-Nrg to soul II soul; see the listings where the best of an evening's clubs are often listed under a particular day.

L'Alibi, Via di Monte Testaccio 44 (tel: 574 3448).

Hangar, Via in Selci 69 (tel: 488 1397).

Jackie O, Via Boncompagni 11 (tel: 488 5457).

Caffè Latino, Via di Monte Testaccio 96 (tel: 574 4020).

La Makumba, Via degli Olimpionici 19 (tel: 396 4392).

RadioLondra, Via di Monte Testaccio 871.

Famous music bar on Via San Francesco a Ripa

THEATRE

You can see Italian classics, plays by lesser-known Italian writers, local versions of popular foreign plays, and avant-garde, alternative works which rejoice under the generic term teatro off. The Teatro Argentina is one of Rome's best-known theatres with a resident company which performs the classics. Teatro Quirino puts on classics and productions brought in from elsewhere in Italy (often with star actors and actresses). You can also see classics at Teatro Valle. In summer the English Puppet Theatre stages dramas by travelling Sicilian and Neapolitan companies. This little theatre is situated in the remains of the Teatro di Pompei.

Teatro Argentina, Largo Argentina 56 (tel: 68 80 4601).

Teatro Quirino, Piazza dell'Oratorio 73 (tel: 679 4585).

Teatro Valle, Via Teatro Valle 23A (tel: 68 80 3794).

English Puppet Theatre, Via di Grotta Pinta 2 (tel: 589 6201).

Festivals

CALENDAR OF EVENTS

January

6 January: **Epifania**. Mass said by the
Pope in St Peter's and Masses in many
other churches.

17 January: **Festa di San Antonio
Abate**. Animals blessed in Sant'Eusebio
all'Esquilino.

February

Sunday to Tuesday before Lent:
Carnevale. Street celebrations (Via
Nazionale and Via Cola di Rienzo in
particular); children dress up.

24 February: **Le Sacre Ceneri**.
Beginning of Lent with Mass and a
procession (sometimes in the presence of
the Pope) at Santa Sabina.

March/April

9 March: **Festa di Santa Francesca
Romana**. Roman drivers bring their cars
to the church of Santa Francesca Romana
to have them blessed by the patron saint
of motorists – a sensible precaution
considering Rome's traffic conditions.

9 April: Rome's official birthday. Torches
are lit on the Campidoglio.

Domenica delle Palme. Palm Sunday is
traditionally celebrated by the Pope who
says Mass in St Peter's Square.

Giovedi Santo. The Pope says Mass in
San Giovanni in Laterano.

Venerdi Santo. Good Friday Stations of
the Cross with the Pope at the candlelit
Colosseum.

Easter Sunday. Papal blessing at St
Peter's.

Late April: **Festa della Primavera.**
Spanish Steps ablaze with azaleas in
terracotta pots.

May

Early May: **International Horse Show**
at Piazza di Siena in the Villa Borghese.
Rose Show at the Via di Valle Murcia
on the Aventine. **Antiques Fair** in Via
dei Coronari (lit with candles at night).
Open-air art exhibition in Via Margutta.

June

First Sunday in June: **Festa della
Repubblica**. Military parade in Via dei
Fori Imperiali.

24 June: **Festa di San Giovanni**. Held
in Piazza San Giovanni in Laterano:
meals of snails and roast suckling pig,
and a fair and firework display.

29 June: **Festa di SS Pietro e Paolo**.
The feast of Rome's patron saints, Peter
and Paul, is celebrated by a Mass in St
Peter's.

Last weekend in June: **Infiorata**. This
flower festival takes place in the town of
Genzano, on the Via Appia,
approximately 30km southwest of Rome
in the Albana Hills. A spectacular,
patterned carpet of flowers covers the
main street leading up to the church.

Late June to late July: **RomaEuropa**.
Festival of film, dance, theatre and
concerts, many performances held in the
grounds of the Villa Medici. Also
Festival dei Due Mondi (see page 150)

July

Last two weeks in July: **Festa dei
Noiantri**: Trastevere's traditional
festival, an open-air party with feasting,
processions and other entertainment.

Beginning of the open-air opera season
in the Terme di Caracalla. Open-air
concerts at Ostia Antica, in the grounds
of Villa Ada and elsewhere around the

city. **Tevere Expo**: Italian products (arts, crafts, food, wine and folk music) in stalls along the Tiber near Ponte Sant'Angelo.
23 July: Bolsena (about 80km northwest of Rome): **Festa di Santa Cristina**. The saint's image is carried in procession through the town, along with tableaux of episodes from her life.

August
1 August: **Festa delle Catene**. At San Pietro in Vincoli, the chains of St Peter's imprisonment are exposed to the faithful.
5 August: **Festa della Madonna della Neve.** At Santa Maria Maggiore, at the 'Gloria' stage of the Mass, flower petals descend on the congregation in re-enactment of a local 4th-century legend.
15 August: **Ferragosto** (Assumption of the Virgin). Main midsummer holiday (many shops and restaurants closed).

September
23 September–7 October: torchlit street and craft fair in Via dell'Orso.

October
Castelli Romani wine festivals.
1st Sunday of October: **Sagra dell'Uva**

in the Castelli town of Marino. Grape festival and wine tasting.

November
22 November: **Festa di Santa Cecilia.** Special services at Santa Cecilia in Trastevere and the Catacombe di San Callisto.

December
Christmas cribs (Presepi) in many of the churches.
8 December: **Festa dell'Immacolata Concezione**. Religious service in Piazza di Spagna, sometimes attended by the Pope.
12 December to 6 January: Children's fair in Piazza Navona, culminating in **Befana**, the 'witch' festival on the eve of Epiphany.
24 December: midnight Masses in churches, especially Santa Maria Maggiore, Santa Maria in Aracoeli and the Papal Mass at St Peter's.
25 December: Mid-morning papal Mass at St Peter's.
31 December: 'Te Deum' outside the Gesù in thanks for the passing year.

The colourful Infiorata, the flower festival in the nearby town of Genzano

Children

*I*t is a truism to say that children delight the Italians, who are always peering into prams, and patting the heads of toddlers. Luckily, in a city where there are few specific entertainments for children, they are generally accepted without question, particularly in hotels and, above all, in restaurants and *trattorie* where great efforts are made to accommodate them. No highchair? Call the waiter. He will construct one from cushions, an old box or the phone books. Few Roman restaurants cater specifically for children, but most menus are easily adaptable – and, of course, the best way to placate most children is with ice-cream or a slab of pizza, both generally available from bars and cafés.

To cater for the needs of energetic but easily tired youngsters you must use your imagination to the full. Here are some hints.

The sacred...

Christmas is a good time to bring children to Rome. In Piazza Navona there is the Befana toy fair (see page 153) where endless stalls sell toys, crib figures and sticky sweet things. In addition, many churches have their own *presepi* (cribs) some of which are huge and enchanting with such delights as running water, miniature trees, stars and

> **DIRECTORY**
> **Ice-cream**: best in Rome: Caffè Giolitti: Via degli Uffici del Vicario 40 (near the Pantheon). Open: 7.30pm–1.30am. Gelateria della Palma: Via Maddalena 20.
> **Toys**: Al Sogno: Piazza Navona 53; Città del Sole: Via della Scrofa 65.
> **Children's haircuts**: Il Parrucchiere dei Bambini: Via Metastasio 17 (tel: 686 5409).
> **Clothes**: Succo d'Arancio: Via dell'Arancio 36; Children's Club: Via della Frezza 61–2

mechanised animals. Relics of the saints – and sometimes even the saints themselves – add a gruesome note to 'boring' tours around the churches, while the **catacombs** (pages 36 and 116) or the displays of bones in **Santa Maria della Concezione** (page 83) might be fascinatingly ghoulish experiences (but beware: they might equally unleash unwanted nightmares). Climb to the roof of **St Peter's** or make a special trip to see the monster-mouth doorway of the building at Via Gregoriana 30, at the top of the Spanish Steps.

The Piazza Navona toy fair

A refreshing dousing

...and the profane

Of all Rome's ruins, the **Colosseum** (page 38) is the most fascinating for children, especially accompanied with tales of wild animals in its arena. Equally, **Castel Sant'Angelo** (page 34) will inspire all kinds of creative imaginings. Slightly older children would probably appreciate the **Museum of Folklore** (page 58), the **Vatican Museums** with their collections of ancient carved marble animals (see Museo Pio-Clementino, page 96) and the **Museo delle Mura** (page 57) which has military appeal. At Bomarzo children would enjoy the **Monster Park** (page 124), which also has an adjacent small playground area with farm animals and swings. Another good outing is to the **Villa Lante** gardens at Bagnaia (Viterbo) with their exotic variety of fountains: don't underestimate the power of water to amuse.

Outdoor fun

The **Zoo** is the obvious choice. It is just one of the attractions of the **Villa Borghes**e which, with its boating lake, and opportunities for hiring rowing boats, riding bicycles (the bike hire point in the Pincian garden has free baby-seats), pony-pulled carts, picnics and generally running amok, is possibly the best of Rome's diversions for children. The **Villa Celimontana** (page 135) has bike trails and cats galore while the **Villa Doria Pamphili** has large open spaces (page 136). If all else fails, you can feed the pigeons in Piazza Navona or fling a coin in the Trevi Fountain and make a wish.

Feeding the pigeons in Piazza Navona

Sport

*A*part from one or two facilities in the Villa Borghese, the centre of Rome has few places to nip into before breakfast for a sharp workout or a quick game of squash. It is different of course if you are staying at one of the grander central hotels or belong to a private club. While it might be possible to jog, cycle or just kick a ball around in parks like the Villa Borghese, Villa Doria Pamphili and Celimontana, you must go slightly further afield to look for any particular sporting interest.

PARTICIPATION SPORT

BOATING

The best boating opportunities are out of Rome, although Villa Borghese has a boating lake and boats for hire. You can hire a boat on Lake Bracciano (40km northwest of Rome), while on Lake Albano, in the region of the Castelli Romani (see page 124), international sailing championships take place. Check listings magazines for details, or contact

---

FORO ITALICO

The concept of physical fitness was dear to the Fascists. Not surprisingly, therefore, the 1930s sports complex, the Foro Italico (at Largo de Bossi 3) became something of a Fascist temple to the cult of the perfect body. Look out for the mosaics on the walls of the main pool – homoerotic renditions of the male body in various states of undress – and the scenes of animals and sea creatures around the *Piscina Pensile*, a pool built for the Fascist youth movement. Mussolini's personal gym – the *Palestra del Duce* – has also survived with its Cubist-style mosaics by Gino Severini. These can be viewed by appointment (tel: 36 851).

---

the **Federazione Italiana Canottaggio**, Viale Tiziano 70, 00196 Rome (tel: 396 6620).

BOWLING

Raucous and rowdy, bowling alleys are an option when your creative juices run dry and you can think of nothing else to do. There is **Bowling Brunswick** at Lungotevere Acqua Acetosa (tel: 808 6147/8), and **Bowling Roma** at Viale Regina Margherita 181 (tel: 855 1184).

CYCLING

There is a serious cycling track, the **Velodromo Olimpico**, in Via della Tecnica. It is also possible to ride in the Villas Borghese and Celimontana and the Villa Sciarra in Trastevere. Rent bikes from: **I Bike Roma** in Villa Borghese car park (tel: 322 5240) and **Collalti**, Via del Pellegrino 82 (tel: 68 80 1084). For further information contact the **Federazione Ciclista Italiana** (Italian Cycling Association), Via Leopoldo Franchetti 2 (tel: 368 57255).

GOLF

Foreigners with membership of a club at home, and an official handicap, are welcome at some clubs for a fee. You need to book in advance. Weekends are sometimes closed to guests, and most clubs shut on Mondays. Rome has four

Fishing in the River Tiber beneath the walls of the Castel Sant'Angelo

golf clubs:

Acqua Santa, Via Appia Nuova 716 (tel: 783 407).

Country Club Castel Gandolfo, Via di Santo Spirito 13 (tel: 931 23 0184).

Fioranello, Santa Maria delle Mole (tel: 713 8213, 713 8058 or 7138212, closed Wednesdays).

Olgiata Golf Club, Largo dell'Olgiata 15 (tel: 378 9141).

For further information, telephone **Federazione Italiana Golf**, Viale Tiziano 74 (tel: 323 1825).

HEALTH CLUBS

For short-term visitors, hotels and private clubs (with a hefty joining fee and possibly a monthly payment) are the only answer if you want to work out in a gym or sweat in a sauna. Daily members are welcomed at the **Roman Sports Centre** in Viale del Galoppatoio 33 (tel: 320 1667) with gym, sauna and swimming pool. The **Centro Internazionale di Danza**, in Via Francesco di Sales 14 (tel: 686 8138), is the place to go for aerobics.

RIDING

Opportunities for riding are rather limited if you are a short-stay visitor to Rome. However, try either the **Centro Ippico Fiano Romano** between Via Tiberina and Capena (tel: 0765/255 019), or the **Riding Club** in Via Tor di Carbone (tel: 542 3998).

The ultimate attainment of physical perfection

ROMAN GAMES AND SPECTACLES

The Games were once part of the daily life of Rome, held regularly throughout the year. Entrance was free and the citizenry crowded eagerly on to the tiers of the amphitheatres to watch the bloodthirsty dramas unfold.

Of the surviving Roman monuments, amphitheatres like the Colosseum (see page 38) are the most imposing. They were the scenes of extravagant and barbaric bloodletting. Augustus tried to interest the populace in Greek games – contests which strengthened the body instead of destroying it – but failed. Then in AD86, Domitian instituted the *Agon Capitolinus*, held in the Circus Agonalis (Piazza Navona, see page 111), with prizes for athletic prowess and artistic accomplishment, such as running and oratory or boxing and poetry. The crowds, addicted to the thrills of the Colosseum, looked on these 'Greek' games as colourless and tame, while the Roman upper classes saw them, with their nudity, as immoral.

Much preferred were the 'live killing matches' held in the Colosseum, gladiatorial combats in which pairs of 'duellers', clad in leather tunics or armour, slashed at each other aiming at mutual extermination.

The hunt spectacles, the *venationes*, were also greatly enjoyed. One version set armed 'hunters' against wild beasts, such as lions, tigers or bears. In another version animals, enraged by prods from keepers, were set against one another. The most repulsive variation on this theme had wild animals, starved in advance, devouring defenceless condemned criminals or, latterly, Christians.

Doomed men provided great sport, particularly in intervals between morning and afternoon 'galas'. Half-naked, they were driven into the arena in pairs; one combatant was armed, the

Top: Roman spectacles were generally vicious
Left: gladiatorial combat was a battle to the death

other defenceless, the first obliged to kill the second. The 'victor' was then himself disarmed, stripped and exposed to an armed newcomer, and so on until a single criminal remained – to have his throat cut.

Then there were the *naumachiae,* sea-battles in which the amphitheatre was flooded. With pitiless realism, armies of condemned criminals were forced to kill each other as they re-enacted some famous sea-battle.

ROMAN CHARIOT RACES

Chariot races were held in the Circus Maximus (see page 121). A race lasted not more than half an hour: four charioteers, each with a team of either two, four or ten horses, were pitted against one another over 14 laps. It was an advantage to run along the *spina* – the shortest distance – and the 'hairpin' bends at either end of the track could be dangerous. In its later stages, the race took on a brutal character, as charioteers tried to wreck each other's fragile chariots. If his cart collapsed or was crushed, the charioteer, who stood with the reins wound around him, had to cut through the reins to prevent himself somersaulting over his chariot as the horses crashed to the ground. If he survived he was given a 'reviving' draught made principally of wild boar's dung. For the winner there was a palm or crown and a substantial financial reward.

Football arouses passions like no other sport

SWIMMING

For a city subjected in the summer months to an often oppressive heat, public swimming baths are few and far between. It is fine for those staying at the grander hotels in the centre, but others will have to take a bus or the metro to find what they want. At EUR, the **Piscina delle Rose** (Viale America 20, tel: 592–6717) is open to the public, and there is the **Piscina Foro Italico** at Lungotevere Maresciallo Cadorna (tel: 321 8591); both are open June to September. Try also **Hotel Shangri-la** (Viale Algeria 141, tel: 591–6441) and the **Hilton** (Via Cadlolo 101, tel:

35091) both of which open their pools to non-residents during the summer months.

TENNIS

Telephone bookings are essential about a week in advance for the public courts at:

EUR: Viale dell'Artigianato 2 (tel: 592 4693).

Foro Italico: Via Gladiatori 31 (tel: 321 9021).

Tennis Belle Arti: Via Flaminia 158 (tel: 360 0602).

Tre Fontane: Via delle Tre Fontane (tel: 592 6386).

Clubs where membership is not needed are:

Centro Sportivo Italiano: Lungotevere Flaminio 55 (tel: 322 4842).

Oasi di Pace: Via degli Eugenii 2 (tel: 718 4550).

For further information, contact the **Federazione Italiana Tennis** (Italian Tennis Federation), Viale Tiziano 70 (tel: 328 3807/324 0578).

SPECTATOR SPORT

CAR RACING
At Valle Lunga on Sundays you can watch Formula 1 and Formula 3 racing. Official trials are also sometimes open to the public on Saturdays.
Autodromo di Roma, Via Cassia, about 34km north of Rome (tel: 904 1417).

FOOTBALL
Rome has two teams, Roma and Lazio. Both first division, they play on alternate Sunday afternoons from September to May at Stadio Olimpico.

Tickets in advance from **Stadio Olimpico**, Via del Foro Olimpico (tel: 399 450) or from **Società Roma**, Via del Circo Massimo 7 (tel: 575 151). For further information, contact the **Federazione Italiana Giuoco Calcio** (Italian Football Association), Via Gregorio Allegri 14 (tel: 84 911).

GREYHOUND RACING
Races are every Wednesday and Thursday evening and on Sunday morning at the **Cinodromo,** Via della Vasca Navale 6 (tel: 556 6258).

HORSE-RACING
Flat races, steeplechases and show jumping all take place at the **Ippodromo delle Campanelle**, Via Nuova 1255 (tel: 718 3143). At the **Ippodromo di Tor di Valle**, Via Mare 9 (tel: 592 683), there are trotting races. In April/May the annual Rome International Horse Show takes place in Piazza di Siena at the Villa Borghese. For further information, contact the **Federazione Italiana Sport Equestri**, Viale Tiziano 74 (tel: 36851).

TENNIS
At the end of May the Italian International Open, a major event with some of the top international players on court, takes place at the Foro Italico, Viale dei Gladiatori 131. For tickets, contact the **Federazione Italiana Tennis**, Viale Tiziano 70 (tel: 328 3807/324 0578).

The magnificent Foro Italico

Food and Drink

*S*urrounded by a rich fertile *campagna,* a region of fields, pastures and vine-yards, Rome is well equipped to feed its population a diet well supplied with fresh vegetables and fruit. Now that it is a proven fact that the Mediterranean diet – sophisticated yet simple and tasty – is an extremely healthy one that everyone would do well to follow, what better place to start than in Rome, situated between the sea and the pastures and mountains?

Italians are noted for their love of food, and most are brought up to be knowledgeable about it. You could even say that Italians live for food, and certainly they spend a lot of money on it. The Italian obsession with food is an old one, as the ancient Romans' gastronomic extravagances show. There is no better entertainment, as far as many present-day Romans are concerned, than a visit to a restaurant. Lunch (*il pranzo*) has always been the day's main meal, though dinner (*la cena*) is gradually replacing it.

At lunchtime nearly everything closes, streets empty and the only visible activity is in the restaurants and cafés. As you lunch, you might see office workers

Dinner, with an inimitable view

WHAT DID THE ANCIENT ROMANS EAT?

'Bathing, wine and Venus wear out the body, but are the real stuff of life' warns an ancient proverb. It might just as well have included food, since eating rendered the ancient Romans incapable after they had enjoyed a hearty evening meal of, say, boiled ostrich or stuffed dormice, asparagus soufflé with quails or roast guinea fowl with sweet and sour sauce. Since the passing of the ancients, tomatoes have arrived from Peru, maize from America, rice from the orient and oranges from Arabia. The Romans of old never ate pasta with a tomato topping because, it is claimed, pasta was first imported by Marco Polo – from China. Yet much of their food was remarkably similar to what is eaten in Rome today, *cecina* (chickpea) cake, or *Lucanica* sausage being obvious examples. They had mustard, oil and wine, and prepared their vegetables much as the Italians do today. But in preference to braising or roasting, meats were boiled until they were bloodless., and might also have been served sugared.

pouring into the restaurant to consume course after course, washed down with copious quantities of local red wine. Their familiarity with the owner of the establishment indicates that this event is a daily occurrence, and you might wonder if any work ever gets done when they return to their desks.

The Food of Rome

In general, the cooking of Lazio – and Rome – is not for the faint-hearted: it is characterised by offal dishes and plenty of oil and garlic, not to mention the rivers of local red and white wine drunk with it. Many Roman dishes are unpretentious and are often the more

Pavement refreshment

tasty as a result. Look out for pasta served with bits of sausage or bacon, *gnocchi* (small potato dumplings, traditionally served on Thursdays) or thick soups containing pasta, vegetables and pulses. Lamb is a favourite, roast, stewed or grilled; indeed lamb's heart, liver, spleen *(milza)* and lungs, heavily seasoned and cooked in olive oil – a dish called *coratella* – is a local speciality you might well encounter on the menu. Other delights not to be missed are local cheeses *(pecorino romano* is a favourite) and the specialities – like *zucchini* (courgette) flowers, dipped in batter and quickly fried – of the Jewish restaurants in the Ghetto. However, if none of these appeal, old favourites from across Italy are also available on most menus.

Best ingredients: the simpler the better

WHAT TO EAT

THE MENU

Antipasto

Most meals begin with a simple *antipasto* – salami or *prosciutto* (cured ham) with pickles, or roasted peppers, grilled aubergine or *carciofi sott'olio* (artichokes preserved in oil). *Antipasto misto* is a mixed plate of olives, salami and a selection of grilled vegetables.

Primo

This is usually pasta, a soup or risotto. In Rome you might have *spaghetti alla carbonara*, with a sauce of beaten eggs, pepper and parmesan, topped with cubes of fried *pancetta* (bacon). Pasta *con vongole* comes with clams, while *cacio e pepe* is with *pecorino* cheese and black pepper. *Maccheroni alla ciociara* comes with a sauce of *guanciale* (rather like bacon), slices of sausage, ham and tomato, and *bucatini all'amatriciana* is long, hollow spaghetti with a sauce of *pancetta*, tomato, chilli pepper and grated *pecorino*. *Penne all'arrabbiata* is short tubular pasta with a chilli sauce hot enough to make you cry, but it is worth a try, as is *fettuccine al burro* – light egg noodles with cream, butter and Parmesan. *Gnocchi* (small dumplings) come with butter, meat or tomato sauce, while Rome's most typical soup, *stracciatella*, a kind of broth with egg, pasta and cheese, should also be tasted. You can just eat the *antipasto* and the pasta courses of the meal, omitting the rest.

Secondo

This is the meat or game *(carne* or *caccia)* or fish *(pesce)* course, sometimes accompanied by lightly cooked vegetables *(verdura)* or a salad *(insalata)*. Offal is the overriding passion of the Roman table. *Coratella* has already been mentioned. *Trippa alla Romana*, thin strips of tripe, are first boiled then stewed for hours with a tomato sauce flavoured with plenty of mint, and there are strange concoctions involving practically every other part of the innards of either calf or lamb. More generally acceptable, however, is *abbacchio,* lamb roasted with lashings of oil and vinegar, sage, rosemary and garlic. With *saltimbocca alla Romana* you get veal pieces cooked with a slice of *prosciutto* and *mozzarella* (or *Fontina*) cheese, sage and a sauce made with Marsala. *Involtini* is slices of meat (usually beef) and *prosciutto* rolled up together then simmered in a sauce with oil, herbs and vegetables, while *brodettato* is a stew of lamb cooked in egg sauce and flavoured with lemon zest. Roman menus also often feature *capretto* (kid) and *porchetta* (sucking pig). The favourite Roman fish is *baccalà,* filleted dried cod which is soaked overnight in cold water then stewed or deep fried. *Zuppa di pesce* is a delicious fish stew. Fish dishes tend to be expensive.

Sweet temptation: the aluring fare of a Roman pastry shop

Contorno

The quality and abundance of products on sale in the Campo dei Fiori market (see page 144) should convince you that the vegetable course will be tasty. Artichokes, beans and aubergines are the Rome favourites though, as elsewhere in Italy, the tomato is omnipresent. Go to the old Jewish Ghetto (see page 53) and eat *carciofi alla Giudia*, artichokes cooked in the Jewish way opened out like a flower and deep fried. Artichokes stuffed with garlic and mint and cooked in oil over a slow heat are called *carciofi alla Romana*. *Fagioli al guanciale* are broad beans cooked with bacon, and *fave col pecorino*, beans with a chunk of *pecorino,* are sometimes eaten at the end of the meal.

Dolci

Most of the cakes. puddings and tarts on offer in Rome are not local specialities and are generally less common in restaurants than in the home. When they do appear, they almost invariably exist as a great slab of something sweet, perhaps drenched in a sweet liqueur and with lots of cream or sweetened *ricotta* and possibly some candied fruit.

Formaggio

Cheese is a better option to end the meal. *Pecorino romano* is a salty ewe's milk cheese, *caciotta* is a soft cheese usually made from ewe's milk, as is *ricotta romana*, though cow's milk is sometimes used these days. Like *ricotta*, *mozzarella* (made from buffalo's milk) is slightly sweet and soft.

EATING OUT

Ristoranti and *trattorie* are virtually interchangeable nowadays. However, in a *ristorante* you would expect the waiters to be wearing aprons and the tables to be covered in neatly pressed, white cloths. A *trattoria* is generally simpler and cheaper, and occasionally there is no written menu: the waiter reels off what the cook has made that day (if you don't understand, look around at what is being eaten and point to something you fancy). The food in a *trattoria* might be inspired by the owner's provenance, which could be anywhere in Italy. In Rome the white *vino della casa* (house wine) is usually more palatable than red. A bread and cover charge (*pane e coperto*), of about L2,000 a head will be added to the bill (*il conto*).

In the Café

One of the most sensible aspects of Italian gastronomic life is the invention of the café, or bar, where breakfast – usually coffee and a *cornetto*, an Italian version of the croissant – is eaten standing up. Cappuccino, coffee with hot milk frothed, is the favoured drink of the early morning. The usual alternative is *caffè latte*, a bigger and more milky cup of coffee. An *espresso*, or simply *caffè*, is generally taken after a meal; with a dash of milk it becomes a *caffè macchiato*. Decaffeinated coffee is *Caffè decaffeinato* – just call it *Hag*. Some of the best coffee in Rome is to be had at **La Tazza d'Oro**, Via degli Orfani 82/84, and at **Sant'Eustachio**, Piazza

Dining on the Pincio

Sant'Eustachio 82 (both near the Pantheon). These places also serve ice-cream, glasses of fresh orange or lemon juice (*spremuta d'arancia/limone*), mineral water (*acqua minerale*) and soft drinks (*alla spina*, from the 'tap', or in a can).

Cafés and bars generally sell delicious selections of filled rolls (*panini*) and sandwiches (*tramezzini*). They come in combinations such as *mozzarella* and tomato, *mozzarella* and *prosciutto* or salami and lettuce. Some bars serve plates of pasta to eat at the bar with a glass of wine.

RESTAURANTS

The price range given in the restaurant listings below refers to an average meal per person including wine, three courses, service and tax; there are three categories:
L = L20,000–L40,000
LL = L40,000–L70,000
LLL = L70,000–L100,000

No telephone numbers are given for inexpensive (L) places, where reservations are not made: you are simply squeezed in wherever possible, or you wait your turn. Some restaurants offer a *menu turistico* (tourist menu) for a fixed price of around L16,000. Restaurants are required to give you a receipt which, by law, you have to retain until you have left the establishment.

Camponeschi LLL

Wonderful location and varied menu with Italian regional dishes. *Piazza Farnese 50 (tel: 687 4927). Closed Sunday and 10 days in August.*

Checchino dal 1887 LLL

Over 100 years old; offal is the speciality. Excellent wine list. *Via Monte Testaccio 30 (tel: 574 3816). Closed August and 1 week at Christmas.*

Da Alfredo all'Augusteo LLL

The 'King of Fettuccine' founded this venerable old restaurant; Alfredo was his name – he was Alfredo I – and Alfredo III, his grandson, is in charge today. See the wall plaster relief panel depicting the apotheosis of Alfredo I: he sits in a chariot being drawn by four huge chargers, a large plate of *fettucine al burro* (his speciality) balanced on his left hand. *Piazza Augusto Imperatore 30 (tel: 687 8734). Open for lunch and dinner; closed Sunday.*

In Rome everything stops for lunch

Da Baffetto L

Busy pizzeria. *Via Governo Vecchio 114 .*

Da Giggetto LL

Menu with Roman 'Jewish' specialities. *Via Portico d'Ottavia 21, Jewish Ghetto (tel: 686 1105). Closed Monday.*

Er Comparone LL

Authentic Roman food, eat outside. *Piazza in Piscinula 47, Trastevere (tel: 581 6249).*

Filetti di Baccalà L
Filled with all types from aristos to workmen. Excellent salt cod snacks. *Largo dei Librai 88.*

Frederico L
Roman cooking. *Borgo Pio, near St Peter's.*

Hosteria dell'Orso LLL
Very 'ritzy'. Has a nightclub upstairs. *Via dei Soldati 25 (tel: 686 4250). Open evenings only; closed Sunday.*

Il Buco LLL
A Tuscan menu. Good service, excellent value. *Via Sant'Ignazio 8 (tel: 679 3298/*

Dallying in the cool

678 4467). Closed Monday and 10–31 August.

Ivo L
Popular pizzeria, eat outside. *Via di San Francesco a Ripa 157, Trastevere.*

La Buca di Ripetta LL
Very popular, Roman food. *Via di Ripetta 36 (tel: 36 12 9391).*

La Fontanella LLL
Eat outside. *Largo della Fontanella Borghese 86 (tel: 687 1092/687 1582). Closed Monday and Saturday lunchtime.*

La Montecarlo L
Pizzeria. *Vicoli 12/13.*

La Rampa LL
Slightly touristy but pleasant, with good food. Sit outside. *Piazza Mignanelli 18, near Piazza di Spagna (tel: 678 2621).*

La Rosetta LLL
Excellent fish dishes. *Via della Rosetta 9 (tel: 686 1002). Closed Sunday, Monday lunchtime, and August.*

ICE-CREAM
An ice-cream shop is called a *gelateria,* and ice-cream is *gelato.* It was introduced to Italy via Sicily by the Arabs, originally as sorbet. You can still buy this crushed, flavoured ice in some *gelaterie,* bars and cafés, and it is immensely cooling on a hot day. *Granita* is very similar: it has fruit juice (lemon is the best), fruit syrup or coffee added to it. If you want an ice-cream cornet *(cone)* or tub *(coppetta),* you can choose a topping of anything from *caffè* to *fragole* (strawberry). *Semi-freddo* is a softer, richer ice-cream. Most *gelaterie* also sell ice-cream by weight for home consumption, and you can sometimes buy *panna montata,* freshly whipped, sweetened cream, to take away. One of Rome's best ice-cream shops is **Giolitti,** at Via degli Uffici del Vicario 40, and another is **Gelateria della Palma** at Via della Maddalena 20.

L'Otello LLL
Typically Roman Food. *Via della Croce 81 (679 1178/678 1454). Closed Sunday.*

Mario LL
Tuscan food, also good pizza. Very popular. *Via della Vite 55 (tel: 678 3818).*

Mario L
Cheap and cheerful. *Via del Moro, Trastevere.*

Osteria Picchioni L
Pizzeria. *Via del Boschetto 16.*

Panattoni L
Pizzeria. *Viale Trastevere 53 (tel: 5800919).*

Piccolo Arancio LL
Lively atmosphere. *Via Scanderburg 112 (tel: 678 6139). Closed Monday.*

Lunchtime on Via della Croce

Pierluigi LL
Excellent food, great location, popular and busy. Eat outside. *Via di Monserrato (tel: 686– 302).*

Piperno LL
Good Roman 'Jewish' specialities. *Via Monte de'Cenci, Jewish Ghetto (tel: 68 80 6629). Closed Monday, August, Christmas and Easter.*

Sabatini LL
Great location, eat outside. Becoming slightly touristy.
Piazza Santa Maria in Trastevere 13 (tel: 582 026). Closed Wednesday.

Sora Lella LL
Wonderful location. Good, simple food if overpriced.
Via Ponte Quattro Capi 16, Isola Tiberina (tel: 686 16 01). Closed Sunday and 30 days over August and September.

WINE

White wines are what are best in Lazio; in fact it is mostly whites that are produced here. None are 'great' wines, but they are ideal for drinking chilled on a hot summer's day. Although some reds are made locally, most of the bottled red wine in Rome comes from elsewhere in Italy.

Some of Rome's finest whites come from the districts around Ciampino Airport, but these are hard to find. The wines of the Castelli Romani (see page 124) are more easily available and include Frascati (dry white – look out for Casal Pilozzo and Colle Gaio), Colli Albani (dry white), Marino (dry white), Colli Lanuvini (dry white), Cori (dry white or red) and Velletri (dry white or red).

One of Lazio's best wines is Est!Est!Est!, a white from around Viterbo. Usually dry and deliciously drinkable, it has a legend attached to its name which should serve as a warning. A German traveller through Lazio was in the habit of sampling the wines of villages he passed through, and he sent his servant ahead to taste the wares, hoping to discover the best. When the servant found something good he would write

Est! ('it is here') on the door so that his master would know where to stop. At Montefiascone he came across a wine so wonderful that the door was emblazoned with *Est!Est!Est!*. The German sat down to drink – and in fact died here from overdrinking, to be buried in the local churchyard.

If you take a trip south to the Parco Nazionale del Circeo (see page 133), ask for a wine from Aprilia, a town on the former Pontine Marshes. Merlot di Aprilia, Trebbiano di Aprilia or Sangiovese di Aprilia are all good, robust table wines sold at very reasonable prices.

Finally, to get a good idea of the wines of the region, or from the rest of Italy, draw up a stool at the bar of **Roffi Isabelli** at Via della Croce 76B. A helpful chalked noticeboard identifies the wines and gives their prices per glass.

Far left: trendy nightspot on Vicolo della Pace
Left: eating out is a social occasion in Italy and is always accompanied by wine

Hotels and Accommodation

*T*here are plenty of hotels in Rome, ranging from the opulent to the basic. The standard is generally high, though there are occasional horrors, and foreign visitors sometimes feel they are paying far too much for what they are getting. The historic centre of Rome is fairly compact and the number of good centrally located hotels is limited. Competition for a room during peak season is stiff, as everybody wants to stay close to the sights and the shopping streets. If you have not booked a room in one of Rome's smaller, central and less pricey establishments well in advance, you may be sorely disappointed.

Making a reservation

Book up two months in advance for a visit in the summer or at Easter or Christmas. The pricier hotels will have faxing facilities for credit card reservations (you will probably be asked to pay a deposit). For cheaper hotels, a telephone call to book and another later, to confirm, is usually sufficient. Say when you expect to arrive. It helps to speak Italian: you are less likely to find your room double booked because of a misunderstanding. Some cheaper places accept only cash or Eurocheques.

The best value is to share a double room. Although it is frowned upon, hoteliers sometimes tell lone travellers that all single rooms are taken and they will have to pay more for a double room.

THOMAS COOK
Traveller's Tip

Travellers who purchase their travel tickets from a Thomas Cook network location are entitled to use the services of any other Thomas Cook network location, free of charge, to make hotel reservations.

HOTEL AMBASCIATORI

The ground floor salon of this huge hotel was decorated in 1926 with frescos by the Venetian painter Guido Cadorin. The murals around the walls depict leading figures from the high society of the day - including, it is said, Mussolini's then mistress, Margherita Sarfatti. Hearing about this, Mussolini ordered the frescos to be curtained over – and thus they remained until after the war.

Prices are per room and are normally posted on the back of the room door. They should include breakfast; if you do not eat it, ask for a reduction. Discounts for long-stay visits and for groups are not unheard of.

Accommodation services

The tourist information offices at Leonardo da Vinci, Termini and the EPT at Via Parigi 5 will make room reservations. If you want to self-cater, **International Services** in Via del Babuino, 79 (tel: 360 00018/19; fax: 360 00037) has a list of studios and apartments, and the UK-based **Landmark Trust** has an apartment adjacent to the Spanish Steps (tel:

Closed shutters on this *pensione* help to keep out the summer heat

0628/82 59 25; fax: 0628/82 54 17 – numbers in the UK). Book well in advance for this. You can obtain lists of residential hotels from tourist information offices. The luxury of these is that you have total privacy along with hotel-style service if you want it.

For budget travellers, some religious institutions have cheap accommodation (try **Domus Mariae**, tel: 663 138 or **Istituto Madri Pie**, tel: 631 967 – both near the Vatican) if you don't mind a night-time curfew and lodging with pilgrims. You should book well in advance, particularly if your visit coincides with a religious event or holiday. Youth Hostels are a cheap alternative: the **Associazione Italiana**

Alberghi per la Gioventù (Youth Hostel Association) is at Via Cavour 44-47 (tel: 487 1152) and the **Ostello del Foro Italico** at Viale delle Olimpiadi, 61 (tel: 323 6279; only holders of AIG or IYHF cards can use this). For your money expect breakfast and a shower as well as a clean bed. Bookings at least 30 days in advance are essential; send a self-addressed envelope for confirmation and be prepared to send a deposit once your booking is accepted (use an international money order). The **YWCA** (Young Women's Christian Association) is at Via C Balbo 4 (tel: 488 3917). For young women under 25, the **Protezione della Giovane** will locate accommodation (Via Urbana 158; tel: 488 1489).

The opulent Lord Byron, a place for star-gazing

HOTELS

Prestigious hotels

The most expensive hotels, like the Hassler-Villa Medici, with its matchless views from the top of the Spanish Steps, or the long established and almost

GRAND HOTEL PLAZA

Hardly noticeable in its position on the Via del Corso, the Grand Hotel Plaza is a magnificent place to stumble into for a reviving cocktail after a hard day's sightseeing. Make for the central salon, adorned with gilded stucco, frescos and Liberty-style stained glass and littered with heavy velvet- and brocade-covered turn-of-the-century furniture to relax in. The hotel, opened in 1860, has an almost baroque extravagance which is thought to capture the mood of optimism following in the wake of the Risorgimento.

indecently luxurious Ambasciatori in the Via Veneto, tend to be located within spitting distance of Piazza di Spagna. Comfortable, opulent, though not necessarily to everybody's taste, these are the places in which to spot celebrities. Ideally situated for shopping and taxis, and close to most of the best restaurants, some of them have the rare luxury of private car parking (the centre of Rome is generally barred to all but residents and essential traffic).

They have private bathrooms, large bedrooms and facilities for carrying out business (faxing, message-taking services, meeting rooms, and so on). A few have recommended restaurants, 24-hour service, beauty salon, sauna and pool. Expect to pay over L400,000 per night for a double room (prices include breakfast, tax and service).

Small but Stylish

Discreet, chic and expensive, these hotels are often hidden in little out-of-the-way cul-de-sacs or squares (the Hotel d'Inghilterra is a good example). Some, like the Sole al Pantheon situated in one of the busiest squares in Rome, have a bland, hardly noticeable façade. You can expect a full range of services but not nearly as many rooms as the hotels in the 'prestigious' category. Expect to pay L300,000 per night upwards (including breakfast, tax and service).

Moderate

Scattered about the city, these hotels are much sought after. Some have a full range of services, others have not. Often it is the view and the location that push up the price. The rooms usually have private showers but there may not be room service or a public bar, just a minibar in the room. Most have direct-dial telephones. Expect to pay from L100,000–L300,000 per double room (prices include breakfast, tax and service).

Cheep and Cheerful

These hotels are generally spartan with no frills. There are a great many in this category; some are good value for money, others are dreadful. Expect not much more than a clean room and a shared shower down the hall (some do not provide towels).

The greatest concentration is around the Via Nazionale and Termini Station, though others are located near

The Hotel Grand is from a gracious earlier era

enchanting locations like Piazza Campo dei Fiori. The latter are popular even if, as occasionally happens, their standards leave much to be desired: some wily owners, knowing that their location and view are 'to-die-for', sometimes slacken up in the cleanliness department. If you are booking from abroad, you could reserve a room for a few days only then, if you do not like it on arrival, look about for something better. This is easy out of season but less practicable at high season when rooms tend to get filled very quickly.

For a double room in this category, expect to pay under L100,000 per night (around L60,000 is a realistic estimate – prices include breakfast). A telephone will be in the lobby, likewise the television.

On Business

*T*he progress of efficient business in Rome can be frustrated by a bureaucracy of Cyclopean proportions. Inefficient communications and the possible inconvenience of having to deal through a third party or agent, exacerbate the situation. However, dealing with officialdom can be eased to a certain extent by embassies, whose commercial departments can advise on the pitfalls of a particular project.

ADVICE AND INFORMATION

The American Chamber of Commerce in Italy
Open: Monday to Friday, 9am–1pm and 3pm–7pm. Via Abruzzi, 25 (tel: 48 26 251).

US & Foreign Commercial Service
They publish useful information on taxation and other matters relating to US businesses in Italy.
Open: Monday to Friday, 8.30am– 11.30am. US Embassy, Via Vittorio Veneto, 119a (tel: 46 74 2240).

British Chamber of Commerce
The 'hows, whys and wherefores' of setting up a business are published in a useful guide.
Open: Monday to Friday, 9am–1pm and 2pm–6pm. Via Sardegna, 40 (tel: 48 26 251).

Connect/Business Guide to Italy
Publishes a useful Business Guide to Italy.

Calling the office

Open: Monday to Friday, 9am–7pm. Via Lorenzo Valla, 40 (tel: 58 09 690).

BUSINESS DRESS AND ETIQUETTE

Always dress the part. You will win no favours (or deals) if you look sloppy. Even if your business is about to disappear down the tube, look confident and dress as though you are worth a million dollars. Remember that Italian business people always dress well.

A degree of formality is also required when addressing your Italian counterpart. Never say *ciao. Buon giorno* or *buona sera* (good morning or good afternoon/evening) and *arrivederci* or *ci vediamo* (goodbye) are the preferred alternatives. Expect to carry out the more important business transactions over a meal and not on the telephone. Even an espresso at a particular bar might become the focus of a deal clinched.

CONFERENCES

With the exception of the large hotels conference facilities are not very well provided for in Rome. **Melograno Congressi,** Large Leopoldo Fregoli 8 (tel: 80 80 892), and **Roma Congressi**, Via Massaciuccoli 12 (tel: 86 04 240), provide a range of services, from basic planning to simultaneous translation.

COURIERS

Speedy Boys, Via Buccari 10 (tel: 37 25 656), deliver locally.

OFFICE SPACE AND EQUIPMENT HIRE

Office space

Short-term modern office space can be found with little difficulty in Rome, some with air-conditioning, secretarial and translation services, and switchboard. Try **Office Hire** at Via Sistina 123 (tel: 47 40 407).

Office equipment

For office equipment (portable phones, filing cabinets and so on) try **Eurocalcolo** at Via Salaria 470 (tel: 86 20 3144).
ATEC Italia, Via Madonna del Riposo 127 (tel: 66 36 741), hire out computers and printers, as do **DEDO Systems**, Via Palestra 11 (tel: 48 81 682).

TRANSLATORS AND INTERPRETERS

Nexus Consulenze, Via Pompeo Magno 94 (tel: 32 33 062), and **Rome at Your Service**, Via Vittorio Emanuele Orlando 75 (tel: 48 45 83), provide a range of services.

WORKING HOURS

Many Roman offices close down at lunch time as workers stage a mass exodus to the nearest restaurant. However, they may well have earned their lunch: many will have begun work at 8.30am and, indeed, will work until 7pm. Generally, businesses and banks (see page 185) close between 1pm and 1.30pm, to open between 2.30pm and 3pm. Always check in advance as working hours vary from place to place. Also remember that punctuality is a concept well known to the Romans.

In general, offices (unless they indicate to the contrary) close down for the whole of August. Even in the weeks leading up to that month it will be difficult to carry out any meaningful business transactions.

Practical Guide

CONTENTS

ARRIVING

Documentation

All visitors, except holders of National Identity Cards, must have a valid passport. Travellers from the US, Australia, Canada and New Zealand require a visa for a stay of more than three months.

In the UK, the Thomas Cook Passport and Visa Service can advise and obtain the necessary documentation – consult your Thomas Cook travel consultant.

By Air

Rome's airports are **Leonardo da Vinci (Fiumicino)** (tel: 65 951) and **Ciampino** (tel: 794 921). See also page 22.

Transfers: from Leonardo da Vinci the most hassle-free way of getting into town is the 30-minute journey by metered taxi (allow two hours at peak times). Trains link the airport directly with Stazione Termini (a 30-minute journey, one train an hour most of the day); and Stazione Tiburtina (a 45-minute trip every 20 minutes from 6am to 1am). On the latter line you can alight at Stazione Ostiense and change to taxi, bus or Metro.

From Ciampino, there is a bus service (ACOTRAL or ATAC) to Anagnina Metro station (service from 5.30am, every half hour until 10.30pm). From there the Metro (Line A) heads towards Termini.

CAMPING

There are no campsites in central Rome; most are a bus journey away. Try:

Capitol, Ostia Antica (tel: 566 2720)

Flaminio, 8km north of the centre (tel: 333 2604)

Nomentano, east of the centre (tel: 41 40 0296)

Roma, 8km north (tel: 622 3018)

Practical alternatives

CLIMATE

From mid-March to May and in September the weather is warm and sunny. In July and August Rome can be baking hot and humid with heavy thunderstorms. November is wet and often very cold. December can be lovely with cold, clear, sunny days.

WEATHER CONVERSION CHART
25.4mm = 1 inch
°F = 1.8 × °C + 32

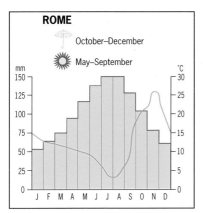

Men's Suits

UK		36	38	40	42	44	46	48
Rest of Europe	46	48	50	52	54	56	58
US		36	38	40	42	44	46	48

Dress Sizes

UK		8	10	12	14	16	18
France		36	38	40	42	44	46
Italy		38	40	42	44	46	48
Rest of Europe		34	36	38	40	42	44
US		6	8	10	12	14	16

Men's Shirts

UK	14	14.5	15	15.5	16	16.5	17
Rest of Europe	36	37	38	39/40	41	42	43
US	14	14.5	15	15.5	16	16.5	17

Men's Shoes

UK		7	7.5	8.5	9.5	10.5	11
Rest of Europe	41	42	43	44	45	46
US		8	8.5	9.5	10.5	11.5	12

Women's Shoes

UK	4.5	5	5.5	6	6.5	7
Rest of Europe	38	38	39	39	40	41
US	6	6.5	7	7.5	8	8.5

Conversion Table

FROM	TO	MULTIPLY BY
Inches	Centimetres	2.54
Feet	Metres	0.3048
Yards	Metres	0.9144
Miles	Kilometres	1.6090
Acres	Hectares	0.4047
Gallons	Litres	4.5460
Ounces	Grams	28.35
Pounds	Grams	453.6
Pounds	Kilograms	0.4536
Tons	Tonnes	1.0160

To convert back, for example from Centimetres to inches, divide by the number in the the third column.

Keeping an eye on the Trevi Fountain

CRIME AND PERSONAL SECURITY

A few commonsense rules should be adhered to.

Leave jewellery at home or in the hotel safe: necklaces or rings are easily removed by an armed thief.

Money and passport should be kept in a money-belt around your waist – preferably out of sight.

Avoid carrying a handbag, camera or video equipment on your shoulder; they can be snatched by thieves on motorcycles.

Never leave valuables in an empty car or on a car seat near an open window.

Watch out for pickpockets – particularly gangs of gypsy children.

CUSTOMS REGULATIONS

As Italy is part of the EU, visitors from other member countries benefit from new regulations introduced in 1993. The amount of duty-paid goods (those bought in local shops) you can take home from Italy is only restricted by notional limits, above which you may be asked to prove that your purchases are for personal rather than commercial use. If you are aged 17 or over you can bring back the following:

800 cigarettes, 400 cigarillos, 200 cigars, 1kg of tobacco, 90 litres of wine, 10 litres of spirits and 100 litres of beer. The allowances for goods bought in duty-free shops (in airports or on board ships and planes), sold free of customs duty and VAT, are unchanged; they also apply to anyone visiting Italy from a country outside the EU.

The allowances here are (per person aged over 17):
200 cigarettes or 100 cigarillos or 50 cigars or 250 gms of tobacco;
1 litre of spirits or 2 litres of table wine and 2 litres of fortified or sparkling wine;
75 gms of perfume.

These limits may vary from time to time so it is best to check when you make your purchase – current limits are posted in duty-free shops.

DISABLED TRAVELLERS

Some tour operators specialise in holidays for the disabled. The **Project Phoenix Trust** publishes a guide, *Access in Florence and Rome*, based on the personal experiences of disabled travellers. Write (enclosing a postal order or cheque for £2.25, to include postage and packing) to: The Project Phoenix Trust, 56 Burnaby Road, Southend-on-Sea, Essex, UK (tel: 0702 466412). Also contact **Radar,** 25 Mortimer Street, London W1, UK (tel: 071–637 5400) for further information.

DRIVING

Accidents

In the event of an accident, exchange insurance information with the driver(s) of other vehicle(s) involved, inform the police and make a statement and inform your insurance company. Most car rental companies provide a form with carbon copy to be filled in by both parties in the case of an accident. See also Breakdown below.

Autostrade

When you join a motorway, you pass through a barrier; stop and press the large red button on the left (driver's side) and you will be issued with a ticket. Hand this in at the booth when you leave the motorway and an illuminated display will tell you what to pay (foreign currency is accepted), unless you hold a Viacard (pre-paid toll card).

Breakdown

Switch the hazard warning lights on immediately and place the red warning triangle 50m behind the vehicle. Find a telephone and ring 116 for the Automobile Club d'Italia (ACI), who will tow any car with a foreign number plate to the nearest ACI-116 garage, free of charge. Use this number too if you have an accident; the ACI will help with police formalities, the exchange of insurance details and finding a garage for repairs.

There are double telephones on the *autostrade:* the one with a picture of a wrench is for reporting mechanical problems and the one with the red cross is for calling an ambulance. The road police (*polizia stradale*) patrol frequently.

Car Rental

The main car rental firms have offices at both airports and at Stazione Termini. They are:
Avis (tel: 478 0150)
Budget (tel: 650 1034/79 34 0137)
Eurodollar (tel: 228 1111)
Europcar (tel: 52 08 1200)

Hertz (tel: 474 0389/65 01 1448)
Maggiore (tel: 854 1620)

To drive a rented car, you must be at least between 21 and 25 (depending on the company) and have held a valid driving licence for a year.

Documents

Unless you hold a pink Euro licence, you need an official translation with your driving licence. If you are driving your own car you will need to carry the registration and MOT documents.

Petrol

Petrol prices in Italy are high. Petrol stations are usually open from 7.30am to noon and 4 to 7pm, Monday to Friday. Many close on Saturday and Sunday, and all close on public holidays, except for *autostrada* service stations.

Some petrol stations display a sign saying 'Aperto 24 Ore'; this means that they have an automatic pump which accepts L10,000 notes. Very few petrol stations accept credit cards. Two types of petrol are sold: *Super* (4-star) and *Super senza piombo* (unleaded). Diesel is sold as *gasolio.*

Recovery

If your car is removed for being illegally parked, call the **Vigili Urbani** (tel: 67 691).

Rules of the road

Traffic drives on the right and the speed limits are 50km/h in built-up areas, 90km/h on secondary roads, 110km/h on motorways and 130km/h on the autostrada. Seat belts must be worn in the front of the car and by children in the rear. Using the horn is prohibited in built-up areas except in emergencies; flash your lights instead as a warning.

ELECTRICITY

220 volts, 50 cycles AC. Two-pin round-pronged plugs are used. Adaptors are widely available.

EMBASSIES

Australia
Via Alessandria 215 (tel: 852 721)
Canada
Via G B De Rossi 27 (tel: 445 981)
New Zealand
Via Zara 28 (tel: 440 2928)
UK
Via XX Settembre 80A (tel: 482 5441)
US
Via Veneto 119A/121 (tel: 46 741)

EMERGENCY TELEPHONE NUMBERS

Police, fire, ambulance 113
Car breakdown (Automobile Club d'Italia; see also page 181) 116
Italian Red Cross (ambulance) 5510
Samaritans 678 9227
Immediate medical assistance (24 hours) **Fatebenefratelli,** Isola Tiberina (tel: 68371)

The Thomas Cook Worldwide Customer Promise offers free emergency assistance at any Thomas Cook Network location to travellers who have purchased their travel tickets at a Thomas Cook location. In addition, any MasterCard cardholder may use any Thomas Cook Network location to report loss or theft of their card and obtain an emergency card replacement, as a free service under the Thomas Cook MasterCard International Alliance.

Thomas Cook travellers' cheque refund (24-hour service – report loss or theft within 24 hours): tel (UK): 1678 72050 (charged at local rates).

LANGUAGE
Pronunciation

A as in father.
E as in egg.
I like e in easy.
O as in ostrich.
U like oo as in food.
C or cc before e or i is pronounced ch, as in church. Otherwise c, cc and ch are prounced k, as in cake.
G is soft as in ginger when followed by i or e, but hard as in go in all other cases.

The accent is nearly always on the penultimate syllable; there are few exceptions to this rule and you will sometimes see them indicated by an accent as in città. Most feminine words end in a (plural e): masculine words end in o (plural i). The definite article is *la* (feminine) and *il* (masculine).

	General
Si	yes
No	no
Grande	large/big
Piccolo	small
Buono	good
Cattivo	bad
Bene	well
Va' bene	everything's fine
Quanto?	how much?
Troppo	too much
Molto	very much
Basta	enough
Aperto	open
Chiuso	closed

HEALTH AND INSURANCE

No vaccinations are required or recommended for Italy, other than to keep tetanus and polio immunisation up to date. AIDS is present (have your own condoms – *profilatici* – and do not rely

Biglietto	ticket			
Entrata	entrance			
Uscita	exit			
Sinistra	left			
Destra	right			
Dove?	where?			
Dov'è?	where is?			
Quando?	when?			
Ferrovie	railway			

Days of the Week

Lunedi	Monday
Martedi	Tuesday
Mercoledi	Wednesday
Giovedi	Thursday
Venerdi	Friday
Sabato	Saturday
Domenica	Sunday

Useful phrases

Parla inglese?	Do you speak English?\
Non capisco	I do not understand
Chi parla inglese?	Who speaks English (here)?
Parla lentamente	Speak slowly
Per favore	Please
Grazie	Thank you
Prego	Please (don't mention it) the invariable response to 'grazie'
Permesso!	Excuse me! (eg when moving through a crowd)
Mi scusi	Excuse me (apology)
Mi dispiace	I am sorry
Niente	It does not matter
Come si chiama?	What is your name/what is this called?

Numbers

Uno	one	**Sette**	seven
Due	two	**Otto**	eight
Tre	three	**Nove**	nine
Quattro	four	**Dieci**	ten
Cinque	five	**Cento**	hundred
Sei	six		

Food and Drink

Acqua	water
Agnello	lamb
Anatra	duck
Arancia	orange
Asparagi	asparagus
Burro	butter
Conto	bill
Fagiolini	green beans
Fichi	figs
Formaggio	cheese
Fragole	strawberries
Manzo	beef
Mele	apple
Olio	oil
Pane	bread
Peperoni	sweet peppers
Pera	pear
Rognoni	kidneys
Sarde	sardines
Spinaci	spinach
Tonno	tuna
Trota	trout
Uva	grapes
Vino	wine (*rosso* red, *bianco* white, *rosa* rosé)
Vitello	veal

on Italians to carry them). Food and water are safe.

All EU countries have reciprocal arrangements for reclaiming the costs of medical services. UK residents should obtain forms CM11 and E111 from any post office in the UK. You are, however, strongly advised to take out private travel insurance to cover all eventualities (available through the AA, branches of Thomas Cook and most other travel agents).

LOST PROPERTY

Report the loss first to your hotel then to the police at the Questura, Via San Vitale 15 (tel: 4686).

Ufficio Oggetti Rinvenuti (the central lost property office): Via Niccolo Bettoni 1 (tel: 581 6040) open 9am–noon.

For items lost on buses and trams: **ATAC**, Via Volturno 65 (tel: 46 951), open 9am–noon.

For items lost on railways: **Ufficio Oggetti Rinvenuti**, Via Marsala 53 (tel: 47 30 6682), open 7am–midnight.

MAPS

Collect a map from the EPT (see page 189). Otherwise some hotels give away street maps, and detailed ones can be purchased from newsstands. For maps of the bus, tram and Metro network, contact the ATAC information office next to Termini in Piazza dei Cinquecento.

MEDIA

Newspapers

There is a wide range of dailies from which to choose: *Il Manifesto* (left-wing) has good 'alternative' arts coverage and listings; *Il Messaggero* (Rome's paper) has good sports coverage; *La Repubblica* (Italy's national daily) is strong on political comment; *Trovaroma* contains listings (out on Thursdays); *Il Tempo* (another of Rome's papers) has local coverage and copious listings; *Corriere della Sera* (quality paper) is possibly Italy's best-written daily; *La Gazzetta dello Sport,* has an exhaustive coverage of sport; *La Stampa* has excellent arts coverage; *La Unita* (once the Communist party newspaper) has good coverage of cultural issues.

L'Osservatore Romano is the Catholic paper, with a weekly edition in English.

Radio

National Radio 1 (RAI, 89.7MHz FM stereo; 1332KHz AM), 2 (RAI, 91.7 MHz FM stereo; 846KHz AM) and 3 (RAI, 93.7MHz FM) strive for quality programmes – news, music, popular programmes – while the local stations such as Radio Centro Suono (101.3MHz FM) play a mixed bag of funky music 24 hours a day and the hugely popular Radio Kiss Kiss Network (97.250MHz FM) provides a non-stop round of chats, music and competitions. Vatican Radio broadcasts in English on 93.3MHz FM and 1530KHz AM.

MONEY MATTERS

The Italian unit of currency is the *lira* (L). There are notes of L1,000, L2,000, L5,000, L10,000, L50,000 and L100,000. Coins are in denominations of L5, L10 (both rare), L50, L100, L200 and L500.

Travellers' Cheques

Thomas Cook MasterCard travellers' cheques free you from the hazards of carrying large amounts of cash, and in the event of loss or theft can quickly be refunded (see page 182 for emergency telephone number, and emergency help locations below). Sterling cheques are recommended, though cheques denominated in US dollars and other major Euro currencies are accepted. Hotels, larger restaurants and some shops accept travellers' cheques in lieu of cash.

The following branches of Thomas Cook can provide emergency assistance in the case of loss or theft of Thomas Cook MasterCard travellers' cheques. They can also provide full foreign exchange facilities; they will change currency and cash travellers' cheques (free of commission in the case of Thomas Cook MasterCard travellers' cheques): Via della Conciliazione 23–25; Piazza Barberini 21A–21D.

Credit Cards
Major credit cards are widely accepted (but check before entering *trattorie* and *pensioni*).

Eurocheques
Accepted for obtaining money (up to L300,000 per cheque – maximum of three cheques – in banks), and usable in some shops, hotels and restaurants.

NATIONAL HOLIDAYS
Banks, offices, schools and shops are closed on:
1 January – New Year's Day
6 January – Epiphany
Variable – Easter Monday
25 April – Liberation Day
1 May – Labour Day
29 June – St Peter's Day
15 August – Assumption
1 November – All Saints' Day
8 December – Feast of the Immaculate Conception
25 December – Christmas Day
26 December – Santo Stefano

OPENING HOURS
Banks
Open 8.30am–1.30pm and 3–4pm.
Bureaux de change
Open 8.30/9am–1pm and 3.30/4 –7/8pm.
Churches
Open from about 7am to noon and 4–7pm. St Peter's, Santa Maria Maggiore, San Giovanni in Laterano and San Paolo Fuori le Mura are open all day.
Museums and Galleries

Most are closed on Monday and Sunday afternoon. Otherwise they are usually open from 9am to 1 or 2pm. In addition, some are open 5-8pm.
Shops and Offices
Normal opening times are 8.30 or 9am to 1pm, reopening at 3.30 or 4pm until 7.30 or 8pm. Many close on Monday morning and all day Sunday. Most bars are open on Sundays while restaurants must, by law, close one day a week (check signs in the window).

PHARMACIES
The following chemists (*farmacie*) are open all night: Brienza, Piazza Risorgimento 44 (tel: 397 38166/397 38183); Cristo Re, Galleria Testa of Stazione Termini (tel: 488 0776); Internazionale (stocks US and UK brands), Piazza Barberini 49 (tel: 482 5456); Piram, Via Nazionale 228 (tel: 488 0754). If your nearest pharmacy is closed, check the list in the window to find which are open.

PLACES OF WORSHIP
Catholic (services in English)
San Clemente (Irish), Via di San Giovanni in Laterano 45–7 (tel: 731 5723); San Silvestro (English), Piazza San Silvestro (tel: 679 7775); Santa Susanna (American), Via XX Settembre 14 (tel: 482 7510).
Other major centres of worship
Anglican: All Saints, Via del Babuino 153 (tel: 679 4357).
Jewish Synagogue: Lungotevere dei Cenci 9 (tel: 686 4648).
Methodist: Ponte Sant'Angelo, Piazza Santo Spirito 3 (tel: 656 8314).
Muslim: Viale della Moschea (tel: 808 2167).
Presbyterian: St Andrew's of Scotland, Via XX Settembre 7 (tel: 487 4370).

POLICE
Emergencies – dial 113
Police headquarters *(Questura)* is at Via
San Vitale 15. They have a helpline for
tourists (tel: 4686, ask for extension
2858 or 2987). Report stolen property
here.

POST OFFICES
Rome's main post office is in the Piazza
San Silvestro (tel: 6771). Open Monday
to Friday, 8am–9pm, and Saturday,
8am–noon, it has 24-hour telephones,
fax and telex, and is the city's *poste
restante* address (address letters to *c/o
Palazzo delle Poste, Roma, Fermo Posta* –
put the underlined surname of the
addressee first). Post offices at Termini
station and Leonardo da Vinci airport
keep the same extended hours.
Telegrams can be sent at any hour of the
day or night (tel: 679–5530). Stamps are
also available from tobacconists
displaying the black-and-white T.

Letters posted at the Vatican City
main post office, or anywhere within the

Go underground

Vatican (Vatican Museums entrance or
Piazza San Pietro – use Vatican stamps
and blue post boxes) will arrive more
quickly than those posted in the
ordinary Italian red pavement boxes.

PUBLIC TRANSPORT

Tickets
Purchase your ticket before you travel,
from bus termini, news kiosks,
tobacconists, and Metro stations. Look
out for places displaying ATAC (bus
and tram) and ACOTRAL (Metro)
signs, or for the green ACOTRAL
kiosks located at main bus stops. Tickets
are also available from the ATAC
information booth in Piazza dei
Cinquecento (facing Stazione Termini;
Metro: Termini).

The Metro
The Metropolitana has two lines – A
and B – and stations are marked by a big
white **M** on a red background. Line A
(red, open 5.30am to midnight) runs
from Ottaviano to Anagnina in the
southeast. Line B (blue, open Monday
to Friday, 5.30am–9pm) runs from
Rebibbia in the northeast to EUR in the
southwest. Basic tickets are valid for a
single journey, but a BIG ticket gives
you a day's travel on all public transport;
monthly passes are also available.

Buses
The main terminus for Rome's bus
service (city buses are generally orange,
out-of-town buses, blue) is in Piazza dei
Cinquecento, and there are major bus
stops *(fermate)* in Piazza Venezia, Largo
Argentina and Piazza del Risorgimento.
Only one (119, a small electric bus) is
able to enter the narrow streets of the
city's centre.

The ubiquitous orange bus is hard to miss

is Rome's largest station – all main national and international lines terminate here – and has a full range of services. It is the focus of the Metro service.

Other stations: **Ostiense** (tel: 575 8748) serves some long-distance north–south trains, and is the station from which to make visits to Ostia Antica. **Roma Nord** (tel: 361 0441) serves Viterbo (2 hours), Bracciano (90 minutes) and other parts of northern Lazio. **Tiburtina** (tel: 43 42 3972), serves some long-distance north–south trains, and trains arriving after midnight stop here.

The *Thomas Cook European Timetable*, which is published monthly at £7.90 and gives up-to-date details of most rail services and many shipping services throughout Europe, will help you plan a rail journey to, from and around Italy. It is available in the UK from some stations, any branch of Thomas Cook or by phoning 0733 268943. In the USA, contact the Forsyth Travel Library Inc 9154 West 57th Street (PO Box 2975), Shawnee Mission, Kansas 66201; tel: 800/367 7982 (toll-free).

The basic fare ticket is valid for just one journey With your pre-purchased ticket, enter at the rear (*salita*) and have the ticket time-stamped in the machine there. Get off through the *uscita* (exit), the middle doors. There are on-the-spot fines (L10,000) if you are caught without a validated ticket. With a bus pass you board at the front. You can get a one-day pass, an eight-day tourist pass (*Carta Settimanale per Turisti*), a one-month pass valid for all lines or a one-month pass valid for a single route. A block of ten tickets (blue as opposed to the regular green ones) saves money. For information, tel: 469 544.

You can buy tickets from the conductor on the night bus – service from midnight to 8am. Information on night services can be found in the *Tuttocittà* supplement of the telephone directory.

Rail Travel

Termini: Piazza dei Cinquecento (tel: 4775; seat reservations: 474 4146). This

Taxis

There are plenty of taxis in Rome. You can pick one up at a rank (the red roof-light must be on): there is a set price for the first three kilometres, then a charge per kilometre thereafter, with surcharges for each suitcase, on Sundays and holidays and at night (11pm-7am). Or you can call a radio taxi (tel: **Radiotaxi** 3570; **Roma Sud** 3875; **Capitale** 4994; **Cosmos** 855 9398). Avoid touting mini-cabs.

Post box

SENIOR CITIZENS

If you are over 60 with identification, you get free entry to: Museo Nazionale Romano, Castel Sant'Angelo, Villa Giulia, Galleria Nazionale d'Arte Antica (Palazzo Barberini). For women over 60 and men over 65 there is 30 per cent discount on the railways with a Carta Argento (silver card), available from mainline stations (not valid 16 June–14 August).

SIGHTSEEING TOURS

City sightseeing tours are provided by ATAC. Bus 110 leaves Piazza dei Cinquecento (in summer, Saturday and Sunday, 10am and 3.30pm; 3.30pm on weekdays; in winter, Saturday, Sunday and holidays, 2.30pm only), its route passing the main sights. It takes about 3 hours. Tickets and information from ATAC in Piazza dei Cinquecento. Other tours with English-speaking guides are offered by: CIT (tel: 47 941); American Express (tel: 67 641); Green Line Tours (tel: 482 7480); Carrani Tours (tel: 474 2501).

Carriages

A *carrozza,* an open carriage, can be hired (from Piazza di Spagna, the Colosseum, Fontana di Trevi, Piazza San Pietro, Piazza Venezia, Piazza Navona) for leisurely drives around the city, costing about L80,000 for an hour. For a longer trip, agree a price with the driver beforehand.

STUDENT AND YOUTH TRAVEL

For reductions on museum and other charges, an International Student Identity Card (ISIC) or a Youth International Educational Exchange Card (YIEE) is useful.

Useful addresses and information centres:
Associazione Italiana Alberghi per la Gioventù (Italian Youth Hostel Association), see page 173.
Centro Turistico Studentesco, Via Genova 16 (tel: 446 791) provides general information. Enquire about reductions, for under-26s, on the State railways. You must have a Carte Verde rail pass.

TELEPHONES

To telephone Rome from the UK dial 010 39 (Italy) + 6 (Rome) + number.

To telephone Rome from elsewhere in Italy dial 06 + number.

To telephone elsewhere in Italy from Rome use regional codes + number.

Country codes from Italy: Australia 00 61, Canada and US 001, New Zealand 00 64, UK 00 44.

The cheapest times to phone within Italy are 10pm–8am Monday to Saturday and all day Sunday. Generally calls abroad from Italy are far more expensive than they are from the UK or US.

Public phones

In Piazza San Silvestro, Palazzo delle Poste has a telephone office (*telefono*), open 24 hours. The desk allots you a booth containing a metered telephone, and you pay afterwards. Bars and tobacconists also have callboxes – look out for the yellow dial sign saying *teleselezioni*. Here you can buy a *carta telefonica* (a pre-paid telephone card) for use in the new orange call boxes from which international calls can also be made.

TIME

Italy is one hour ahead of GMT in winter, one hour ahead of BST in summer, but as British clocks go back for winter a little later than in Italy, there is a short time in October when times are the same. New York and Montreal are six hours earlier than Italy, and Sydney eight hours later than Italian time in the summer.

TIPPING

Bars
For speedy service, drop L200 in the plate on the counter.

Custodians
If anything is specially opened for you, always give the custodian something upwards of L1,000.

Restaurants
Some automatically add a 10 to 15 per cent *servizio* (service charge), others do not: read the bill. In addition, waiters expect a small tip.

Taxis
Add 10 per cent on to your fare.

Others who expect tips are hotel porters, cinema and theatre ushers, airport and railway porters and lavatory attendants.

TOILETS

Public conveniences are scarce in Rome other than at stations and larger

Roman toilets of culture

museums. Most bars have a *gabinetto* or *bagno:* some are shared, others have one for each sex – *signori* (men) and *signore* (women). The sign which reads *guasto* means that it is out of order.

TOURIST INFORMATION

For information about Rome, hotel reservations, listings, maps and itineraries:

EPT (Rome Provincial Tourist Board), Via Parigi 5 (tel: 488 3748), open Monday to Saturday, 8am–7pm; Leonardo da Vinci airport, International Arrivals Area (tel: 65 01 0255), open 8.15am–7pm; Stazione Termini (tel: 487 1270), open 8am–7pm.

For information about the rest of Italy: **ENIT** (Italian National Tourist Board), Via Marghera 2 (tel: 497 1282), open 9am–5.30pm, Monday to Friday.

ACKNOWLEDGEMENTS

The Automobile Association wishes to thank the following photographers and libraries for their assistance in the preparation of this book.
J ALLAN CASH PHOTOLIBRARY 19, 64, 65a, 65b; MARY EVANS PICTURE LIBRARY 10, 130, 158/9a, 158/9b, 158/9c, 159; JIM HOLMES 15, 39, 57, 149, 170; IMAGOS CHRIS COE 153; NATURE PHOTOGRAPHERS LTD 132 (R Smith), 133a (K Carlson), 133b (M Gore); PICTURES COLOUR LIBRARY 37b; SPECTRUM COLOUR LIBRARY 100; ZEFA PICTURE LIBRARY 92a, 92b, 93a, 93b.
71 Keats' Grave – reproduced by kind permission of the London Borough of Camden from the Collections at Keats' House, Hampstead.
The remaining photographs are held in the Automobile Association's own photo library (AA PHOTO LIBRARY) and were taken by Jim Holmes with the exception of pages 29b, 36, 37a, 50, 51a, 62, 63, 82b, 83, 85, 86, 87, 99, 102, 103, 139a, 141, 162, 164, 165, 166 and 171, which were taken by Dario Mitidieri, the cover, inset, spine and pages 1, 2, 5, 45, 73, 127, 129 and 180, which were taken by Clive Sawyer, 28, 122, 124, 125, 126 and 128, taken by Antony Souter, and pages 47a, 53, 79, 117, 147b, 163, 168, 173, 174, 175, taken by Peter Wilson.

The Automobile Association would also like to thank Paolo Diamante and the Automobile Club d'Italia for their kind assistance in verifying details in the Practical Guide.

CONTRIBUTORS
Series adviser: Melissa Shales **Designer:** Design 23 **Copy editor:** Audrey Horne
Verifier: Kerry Fisher **Indexer:** Marie Lorimer